30 DAYS TO A MORE POWERFUL BUSINESS VOCABULARY

30 DAYS TO A MORE POWERFUL BUSINESS VOCABULARY

The **500** Words You Need to Transform Your Career and Your Life

DAN STRUTZEL

MEDIA

Published 2020 by Gildan Media LLC
aka G&D Media
www.GandDmedia.com

Certain elements of this book were previously published in a book titled
Word Power for Business, published by Gildan Press.

Front Cover design by David Rheinhardt of Pyrographx

Interior design by Meghan Day Healey of Story Horse, LLC

Library of Congress Cataloging-in-Publication Data is available upon request

ISBN: 978-1-7225-0323-9

10   9   8   7   6   5   4   3   2   1

Contents

Banking and Finance

Negotiation

Marketing

Sales

Entrepreneurship

E-Business

Human Resources

Leadership

Remote Working

Foreword

Welcome to this book, and to a learning experience that can change your life forever. With what you discover in the pages ahead, you will learn more, earn more and get promoted faster than perhaps you ever thought possible

I'm Brian Tracy, personal development speaker, and author of more than over 86 books. I have produced more than 1000 audio and video learning programs, including *Eat That Frog* and *No Excuses: The Power of Self-Discipline*. Over the past 45 years, I've given more than 5,000 talks and seminars to more than five million people in 84 countries.

I have had the privilege of teaching some of the most successful professionals across the globe how to achieve greater success and happiness in their careers and personal lives. Throughout these years, I have noticed that nearly all of them, with very few exceptions, share a common trait. It's the trait that my late friend and mentor, Earl Nightingale, called "The One Thing You Can't Hide."

That special trait is an *extensive vocabulary*. They have a collection—think of it as a great tool chest—of words that they use to become a world-class communicator, and to achieve the goals that they strive to achieve in life. They use these words to negotiate great deals, persuade their customers to make buying decisions, inspire their employees to achieve their company's mission, connect in an intimate way with their spouse, and to encourage their children to have faith in themselves.

A great vocabulary contains the building blocks you need to build a great career. And that's why I'm so excited to introduce you to this all-new book, published by G&D Media: *30 Days to a More Powerful Business Vocabulary: The 500 Words You Need to Know To Transform Your Career and Your Life*.

The author of this book, Dan Strutzel, is a man I've known for over twenty-five years, and a long-time veteran of the personal development industry. As the Vice President of Publishing at The Nightingale-Conant Corporation, Dan was responsible for publishing some of my most successful audio and video programs.

In addition to myself, Dan has worked "up close and personal" with several hundred personal development authors and speakers—some of the most gifted communicators in the world. As a result, Dan has had a unique opportunity to study their communication styles. As a person with a great vocabulary and ability to communicate himself, he was responsible for making those top communicators even better. And I'm convinced that he'll be able to do the same for YOU as well.

As a graduate of The University of Notre Dame, and the President of Inspire Productions, Dan is uniquely qualified to "inspire" you to build a rich and dynamic vocabulary of your own.

I had the pleasure of introducing you to Dan's first vocabulary book, *30 Days to a More Powerful Vocabulary*, which has become a national best-seller. In this all-new book, focused specifically on the business world, you'll learn the words you need to advance to the next level in your career—whether you are a leader, a manager, a top executive, an entrepreneur or a "solo-preneur."

The words you'll learn to master here, with Dan's unique 30-day learning system, will give you a leg up on your competition and help you to advance to the next level in your career. This book even includes a new chapter on "*Remote Working*" to help you to master the vocabulary of a "post-pandemic" business world.

And now, it's my pleasure to introduce you to my friend, Dan Strutzel.

—Brian Tracy

Introduction

Hello and welcome to *30 Days to a More Powerful Business Vocabulary*, an introduction to the vocabulary of business. As we look at the language business people use, the words they say and how they say them, we will gain insights into how business works today. And by focusing intensely on this goal of improving your business vocabulary over a 30-day period, you can not only achieve your goal more efficiently, you will establish a habit of enhancing your vocabulary-building muscles that, with commitment, will last a lifetime.

Business is just like any sector or topic with its own language, customs, codes, and terminologies. Different aspects of business can have their own distinctive terminology, which can also overlap, For instance, words and phrases from the realm of sales can also apply to management or finance under a variety of circumstances.

This book presents five hundred words and short expressions from a variety of different business categories. Some of these words and phrases will no doubt be familiar to you, at least in the sense that you may have heard them before. Others may be entirely new. But there's a good chance you may be encountering this material for the first time in a business context. Some terminology may seem academic and technical—yet this is also important to understand for anyone who really wants to see how the worlds of money and commerce function.

Each chapter of the book introduces approximately twenty-five words. First presented is an informal conversation using the vocabulary in context. Then we discuss each word or phrase and its definition. Finally, we reinforce the word and its meaning with another example in a sentence. There are four chapters on banking and finance, four on marketing, and four on negotiation. Other chapters focus on sales, entrepreneurship, human resources, e-business, leadership, and remote working. The book's intention is to be entertaining, informative, and inspirational and to encourage you to learn more about the topics that are covered.

There certainly is a lot more to discover. You will hear familiar words appearing in a new context along with strange or technical sounding words and phrases. This is certainly not "the last word," so to speak, on the vocabulary of business, but it's a good start toward a wider and deeper understanding. If you return to the book more than once and gain some real familiarity with the language, you can go on to use terms like "SWOT matrix" and "roll the tortoise" in your own everyday vocabulary.

Along with the informative effect of these chapters, one other aspect of the book deserves special attention. You may be amazed to see just how much the language and thinking styles of high technology have become the mainstream of business communication. Perhaps one could argue that this isn't surprising in a world where at least half the people on any busy street are talking on or looking at their smart phones. On the other hand, strange as it may seem, two decades ago not many people even owned a smart phone. Now the smart phone owns us. Technology has not only changed the physical means of our communication, but also the content of what we say and how we think. As you'll see in these chapters, today's business discourse is irreverent, uncensored, ironic, and unsentimental. It would also have been completely incomprehensible a few years ago. As the world changes, language changes with it—and both are changing very fast.

Thank you for reading and please enjoy the book. It's like putting socks on an octopus, and if you don't know what that means right now, you will know very soon.

How to Use The 30-Day Program

My promise to you, as described in the title of this book, is to enable you to add the 500+ words that you will learn to your own vocabulary, available for your daily use, within 30 days. This is an ambitious goal—and one that is highly achievable if you simply commit to following the program. You will find this is a systematic process for learning and then reviewing the words on a daily basis. You will notice that each chapter suggests the specific days in the 30-Day Program to focus on those words.

First Intensive Review

On the suggested day, read the chapter in full when you are in a place where you can give it your full attention. Then, go back and read everything out loud.

Next, review again in an "intensive" way. Research into what is called "super-learning" has demonstrated that if you study in a relaxed and distraction-free state of mind, your retention of the information increases dramatically. For this "intensive" learning, find a quiet place where you will not be disturbed. Sit on a comfortable chair or couch, close your eyes, and slowly breathe ten times—in through your nose and out through your mouth. Count down each breath slowly from ten to one. When you get to one you should be very relaxed, focused and distraction-free, perfect for an "intensive" review of the information. Finally, your fourth and final review for the given day will be within five minutes before bedtime. You might want to keep this book by your bedside, so you can review just before going to sleep.

Super-Learning

Why do I suggest these four review sessions, with such specific methods and times? Research into super-learning looks at how your subconscious mind is best enabled to create new memories. Your subconscious mind is the part of your brain which stores long-term memories for retrieval at a moment's notice. Three important factors that heighten the ability of your subconscious to receive learning are: 1) the use of repetition, 2) being in a state of relaxed alertness, and 3) reviewing just before drifting off to sleep. If you approach the words in these super-learning ways—reading and speaking them out loud, along with their definitions, at least four times on the assigned day—after 30-days you will find these new vocabulary words have become a permanent part of your way of thinking, writing and speaking. Remember, the 30 days that follow will pass whether you implement this program or not. And, given that this review time will take no more than 15 minutes per day, it will have little to no impact on your daily schedule. Why not take the next 30 days to see what amazing things you can accomplish? My hope is that this practice will be so valuable, that you continue it well beyond 30-days.

Essential Review

Lastly, a word about how the assigned days and categories are organized. You will move along though each chapter consecutively, day-by-day, and then return to those chapters later. There is a very specific reason why the *30-Day Program* is organized this way, rather than two consecutive review days back-to-back. While repetition is important in learning, research has shown that "spaced repetition" is even more so. When you repeat your review after a period of time has passed since the *First Intensive Review*, the words have time to settle into your subconscious, long-term memory and the retention is actually more effective. For these later, *Essential Reviews*, you will be studying multiple chapters on the same day. You will be familiar with the words upon your second review, and should be able to move through the material much more quickly.

In summary, here's how to proceed with the *30-Day Program*, step-by-step.

On the suggested day for each chapter:

1. Read the entire chapter from beginning to end.
2. Immediately afterward, go back and read everything out loud—the list of words, definitions and "sentence definitions."
3. Immediately afterward, go back and review the list of words again with the "intentional process" described above.
4. Five minutes before bedtime, review again, just before going to sleep.

*   *   *

I have included *The 30-Day Program Worksheet* as an Appendix to help you keep track of your progress. The worksheet outlines the program and is your checklist as you move through the 30 days. You may wish to look at it now, before beginning with the first chapter.

Tips for a More Powerful Business Vocabulary

The core of the **30-Day Program** I've outlined above is to review the assigned chapter four different times on its given day.

Here are additional tips you can use during the program and hopefully, for the rest of your life. Adding any one of these ideas to your vocabulary-building project, will further expand your business vocabulary and bring you the fluency you seek.

First, *read* as many business books as you can. Strive to read topics in your particular field, as well as business titles on skills and topics where you need the greatest growth. If you are looking for a place to start, begin with long-time business classics such as *The Effective Executive* by Peter Drucker, *The Goal* by Eliyahu Goldratt, *Grit* by Angela Duckworth, *The Seven Habits of Highly Effective People* by Stephen Covey, *Dare to Lead* by Brené Brown or *Good to Great* by Jim Collins. But, the important thing is to read as much as you can. It's true that some reading materials will teach you more than others—but the purpose of reading everything is to make reading a deeply ingrained habit. If you read enough, you'll see important vocabulary words used in context—and that's the best way to learn words for the long term.

The more words you are exposed to, and the more ways you see them used, the better business vocabulary you will have. Studies have shown that the majority of new words are learned from context. To improve your context skills, watch how words are actually used.

After you complete this book, pay close attention to the words you learned here while you read further. See how they are actually put to work. Give special attention to words you don't know, or that you've never seen before. Try to figure out their meanings from context, but don't stop there. Look up all the words you're unfamiliar with. Challenge yourself to read difficult business material so that you'll encounter lots of new words.

Second, *practice, practice, and practice* some more. Make a determined effort to use the words you're learning. Vocabulary is not just an academic exercise. Learning the definition of a word alone won't prevent your forgetting it—you will forget a word if you don't use it. The **30-Day Program** is designed to make practicing a habit. Research has shown that 10 to 20 repetitions are needed to really make a word part of your vocabulary. Once you have completed the **30-Day Program**, experiment with other forms of practice. For example, it helps to write words down. Even if you feel confident that you know certain words, writing them on index cards can be a really effective strategy. Write the definition of the word, and also a sentence that shows how the word is used—just as we do in the **30-Day Program**. Some words can be used as both nouns and verbs, so make up examples of both uses. Review your index cards to make sure you're using the words you've learned, and to see if you've forgotten how any of them are used. As soon as you learn a new word, start using it in conversation. We use this technique in the *30-Day Program*—it's a natural way of learning new vocabulary and it's the way we acquired most of our language to begin with!

Third, *make up as many associations and connections for words as you can.* Try to relate the word to other words you already know. For example, the word "objective" when used as a noun in a business context means a goal, an aim or a strategic position. Make a mental list of things in a business (perhaps the business or organization for which you work) that could be considered objectives. Create an imaginary image for the word that dramatizes its meaning, like "The primary objective for our sales team is to sell $10 million dollars of our product in the next year."

Making up vivid sentences like that is actually a form of mnemonics, which means "memory tricks." For example, the late Zig Ziglar, a great speaker and sales trainer, used to joke about the word "assume," I saying it is always dangerous to assume something, because it can "make an ass out of you and me." See how many of these mnemonic tricks you can come up with.

Fourth, have *fun* with words. Play games like Scrabble and Boggle. Do crossword puzzles. You can even do word puzzles on your cell phone. Taking tests can challenge your knowledge of words, and help you see your progress in your vocabulary. Books of practice SAT tests are especially good.

The fifth and final tip—almost too obvious, but it's really not. In fact, it may be the most important tip of all for building your vocabulary. *Look up words in the dictionary.*

Thanks to cellphones, we all have the power of instantaneous look-up right in our pockets. But for enhanced, intentional, super-learning, I suggest you give the old-school, hard copy or paperback version of the dictionary a try. The act of physically looking up a word requires more focused attention and has been shown to improve retention. And you just might encounter other new words along the way. A portable, paperback dictionary you carry around with you is your super power for vocabulary-building. Many of the words you'll encounter in this program may be entirely new to you. Others may seem familiar—but are actually new, because you see and hear them used in an entirely different way. So keep your eyes open, keep your mind open and you'll be glad you did.

Banking and Finance
PART ONE
(DAY 1, DAY 21)

Banking and finance are the foundation of every business, whether large or small. Yet "money people" are sometimes seen as only a necessary evil in business. The innovators and inspired leaders get the credit, but sooner or later, every business needs financing, and everyone in business needs some familiarity with the language and communication style of the custodians of cash and credit. In four chapters on banking and finance, we will seek to gain some of that familiarity. Here are the words and phrases for the first of these chapters, followed by a conversation and then the definitions.

1. CFO
2. Exposure
3. Capital
4. Arrearage
5. Sandbagging
6. Overhead
7. Physical plant
8. Accounts receivable
9. Accounts payable
10. Phoning it in
11. CEO
12. Subsidiary
13. Bean counting
14. Quarterly reviews
15. Interface
16. Incentive
17. Cautionary tale
18. ROI
19. Woolly mammoth
20. Whale
21. Per se
22. Metric
23. Fiscal year
24. Ratios
25. Trend lines

Here's a conversation about the role of financial executives and accountants in the environment of a large corporation. As someone one said, "You can't live with them and you can't live without them."

Sometimes executives on the financial side of large corporations don't get respect as innovators or generators of profits. Has that been your experience at all?

Well, **CFOs** definitely participate in the decision making process that generates revenue. But other people on the financial side may be less involved, so sometimes they do get less respect.

Why does that happen?

For one thing, financial people can seem hesitant. They have to speak out against reckless **exposure**. They see their job as trying to preserve **capital** rather than growing capital. And of course they're generally very averse to **arrearage**. That kind of caution can be mistaken for **sandbagging**.

Sometimes finance people are seen as nothing more than **overhead**, as if they were part of the **physical plant**. It's as if they just mechanically process **accounts receivable** and **accounts payable.** But you can't run a company without those functions. It's not just **phoning it in.**

So how can a person on the financial side advance in a corporate environment?

Being well-connected is part of it. Make yourself useful to the **CEO**. That way, when a **subsidiary** manager makes a proposal, the CEO can say, "Why don't you talk to my friend in the **bean counting** department?"

Also, let people know that their **quarterly reviews** will be affected by how they **interface** with finance. They need to have an **incentive** to take you seriously.

*What kind of feedback should a good finance person offer, beyond **cautionary tales** about risk and debt?*

Well, **ROI** is always the basic goal. But how do you define ROI? Can you precisely quantify the difference between a **woolly mammoth** and a **whale**?

Numbers **per se** are not always the best **metric**—for example, only comparing this **fiscal year** to the last one can be deceptive. **Ratios** are more informative. For instance, the ratio of sales expenses to sales income can be revealing. **Trend lines** can also give you information that raw numbers don't provide.

....

CFO

Definition: CFO is an abbreviation for Chief Financial Officer. In a business or corporation, the CFO is a senior executive with overall financial responsibility for the entire enterprise. This includes planning new projects, supervising current ones, and dealing with any remaining concerns from projects in the past. The CFO works closely with the Chief Executive Officer and is usually the second highest ranked executive in a company.

Sentence Example: The new CFO needed some time to become acquainted with our firm's eccentric accounting methods, which aren't the methods taught in business schools.

EXPOSURE

Definition: Exposure is the possibility or probability of financial damage to an individual or a company. Exposure can be attached to investments, hiring decisions, expansion possibilities, or virtually any other change in the way a company does business. Exposure is typically something that companies seek to avoid, but since the possibility of gain is often directly tied to the presence of exposure, risk can also be a sign of opportunity.

Sentence Example: Introducing a new sugary candy bar to the retail market carries significant exposure, because the public is becoming more conscious of weight-related issues.

CAPITAL

Definition: Capital is the wealth of a business or individual. Capital can exist in many forms, including cash, real estate, or lines of credit. Generally speaking, capital refers to assets that are readily available for investment purposes.

Sentence Example: She put significant capital into long term investments, which she looked upon as a personal retirement fund.

ARREARAGE

Definition: Arrearage refers to debt owed by one party to another, with the expectation that the borrowed amount will be paid back. Usually the time frame for repaying arrearage is clearly stated, and usually there is interest paid on the debt's original amount. Many businesses depend heavily on debt and couldn't survive without it—although excessive arrearage in a company is viewed as a significant weakness by potential buyers or investors.

Sentence Example: In order to clear his arrearage as soon as possible, Brian decided to pay twice the minimum amount on his monthly credit card bills.

SANDBAGGING

Definition: Sandbagging, in business slang, refers to a strategy of gaining an advantage by making something seem more difficult or expensive than it actually is. Deadlines, contracts, share prices, and salary issues are all vulnerable to sandbagging. Sandbagging is almost a universal practice in American business, and may be even more common in other parts of the world.

Sentence Example: William sandbagged the completion date for his business plan in order to go skiing in Aspen.

OVERHEAD

Definition: Overhead refers to the costs in money or other assets that are required to sustain a business—and that do not directly contribute to the goods or services that the business offers. Rent, payroll, insurance, and utilities are typical overhead expenses.

Sentence Example: When apartment rents began to rise in the neighborhood, overhead for restaurants and clothing stores also went up.

PHYSICAL PLANT

Definition: The term "physical plant" refers primarily to the buildings in which a company does business. It can also refer to specific aspects of the buildings, such as heating and air conditioning units or plumbing issues.

Sentence Example: At some universities the football field is nothing more than an open field of grass, but at Ohio State the stadium is a major component of the physical plant.

ACCOUNTS RECEIVABLE

Definition: Accounts receivable refers to funds owed to a business by other businesses or individuals, and that are legally enforceable and collectable. Accounts receivable can take the form of unpaid invoices, promissory notes, or even oral contracts under certain circumstances.

Sentence Example: The company did not have much cash, but there were significant accounts receivable on the balance sheet.

ACCOUNTS PAYABLE

Definition: A company's accounts payable are simply its unpaid bills. This can include money owed to suppliers, payroll, and taxes. The ratio of accounts receivable to accounts payable is a common indicator of a company's financial strength, and also of the quality of its management.

Sentence Example: The potential investor lost interest when she looked at the accounts payable column on the company's financial statement.

PHONING IT IN

Definition: "Phoning it in" is a business slang phrase that denotes half-hearted effort or laziness. It means taking the easy way out or cutting corners, rather than fully meeting the demands of a responsibility. "Phoning it in" is usually intended as a criticism.

Sentence Example: After a while you can tell the difference between a rep who really wants to make the sale and one who's phoning it in.

CEO

Definition: CEO is an abbreviation of Chief Executive Officer, the highest ranking manager in the day-to-day operation of a business or corporation. The CEO is generally held responsible by the Board of Trustees for the company's success or failure, although it is not uncommon for a CEO to also function as Chairperson of the Board.

Sentence Example: When Steve Jobs returned to Apple after being fired by John Scully, he regained the title of CEO.

SUBSIDIARY

Definition: In a business context, the word subsidiary denotes a business controlled by another business, generally through ownership of more than fifty percent of the subsidiary's stock. The New Yorker magazine, for example, is a subsidiary of the Conde Nast publishing company.

Sentence Example: Jennifer was surprised to learn that the American perfume company was a subsidiary of a Japanese conglomerate.

BEAN COUNTING

Definition: Bean counting is a business slang term for accounting and other strictly finance-related concerns. A bean counter is a finance executive who may be depicted as dull or unimaginative compared to personnel in other areas of management. Bean counting is considered important, but something of a necessary evil.

Sentence Example: In order to refute his reputation as a boring bean counter, Maurice wore a Santa Claus hat to the company Christmas party.

QUARTERLY REVIEWS

Definition: A quarterly review is a performance evaluation that takes place four times a year, in which a manager discusses the strengths and weaknesses of an employee. The results of quarterly reviews can influence the compensation package of an employee, including a year-end bonus, and can also affect an employee's overall future with the company.

Sentence Example: After having a lot of success recently in her new role, Janice was looking forward to her quarterly review.

INTERFACE

Definition: Interface refers to an imaginary boundary line in which two or more departments in a company interact and exchange information. The word derives from computer terminology. Software interface, for example, includes commands, codes, and applications that enable different programs to communicate with each other and with the computer's operating system.

Sentence Example: Because interface between accounting and human resources was weak, the new manager was paid far more than the company could afford.

INCENTIVE

Definition: In business, an incentive is a reward offered to an employee or to a customer for a certain desired behavior. For an employee, a typical incentive might be a financial bonus for meeting an annual sales goal. For a customer, it could be a discount for a payment in cash, or for buying within a certain time period. Incentives can also take the form of cruises or vacations, or discount coupons for a restaurant.

Sentence Example: Paul was surprised to learn that a cruise to Alaska is a more powerful incentive for most employees than a cash bonus at Christmas.

CAUTIONARY TALES

Definition: A cautionary tale is a somewhat ironic term for a business anecdote intended to warn the listener against making a certain mistake. Many companies have cautionary tales that pertain to specific executives or other employees. Cautionary tales are often humorous, but with an important message as well.

Sentence Example: Rachel told the new hire a cautionary tale about what happens to people who don't make friends with the receptionist.

ROI

Definition: Return on Investment (ROI) expresses the earning power of assets as a ratio of the net profit against capital expended on a project. Simply put, ROI tells what the company got for what the company spent in terms of time, effort, and money.

Sentence Example: Although Ron's contract seemed to be fair, he spent so much time on the job that his ROI was very low.

WOOLLY MAMMOTH

Definition: In business slang, a woolly mammoth is a client so large that the company can be sustained by that client for a long period of time. While woolly mammoths are much sought after, they can also be dangerous if the company neglects to develop any other clients.

Sentence Example: Bank of America was a woolly mammoth for Brian's ad agency, until he suddenly lost that account.

WHALE

Definition: Whale is a slang term for a client that provides major revenue, but lacks the long-term sustainability of a woolly mammoth. Whales often appear suddenly and are willing to pay a premium rate for work done under a tight deadline. Companies must decide whether to put aside other work in order to land the whale.

Sentence Example: The plumbing company sandbagged some residential customers in order to service a whale with a broken water main.

PER SE

Definition: Per se is a Latin phrase that literally means "by itself" or "in itself." It is often used in business jargon as an emphasizer in a sentence, although it could be eliminated without changing the meaning of the sentence.

Sentence Example: Ben's management skills were not outstanding per se, but he was promoted because his father owned the company.

METRIC
Definition: A metric is a numerical standard by which efficiency, quality, or progress can be measured in a business environment. Accurate metrics are especially important in situations where quantitative analysis may be difficult, as in leadership skill development or relationships with customers.

Sentence Example: Since there was no metric for measuring how a live assistant's voice sounded on the telephone, Nora installed an electronic voicemail system.

FISCAL YEAR
Definition: A fiscal year is any twelve month period, which may or may not correspond to the calendar year, at the end of which a company determines its financial condition.

Sentence Example: Because the firm's fiscal year ended in October, management deferred some income until November for tax purposes.

RATIOS
Definition: A ratio is the result obtained by dividing one number or quantity by another. Ratios are the simplest mathematical expression of important relationships that may be hidden in a mass of data, and they can reveal meaningful comparisons.

Sentence Example: The ratio of Ellen's time spent at the water cooler compared to her monthly sales performance was brought up at her quarterly review.

TREND LINES
Definition: A trend line is a line on a chart whose direction indicates a pattern of activity within a certain period of time. Trend lines are useful visual expressions for issues such as profit and loss, customer retention, or employee productivity.

Sentence Example: At the company's shareholder meeting, trend lines projected on a large screen were greeted with spontaneous applause.

Banking and Finance
PART TWO
(DAY 2, DAY 21)

Even the most experienced private equity executives and hedge fund managers were once beginners. This second chapter on banking and finance looks at that industry's terminology from a beginner's perspective. It may seem intimidating and obscure at first, but listen closely. As the saying goes, money talks.

1. Investment portfolio
2. Funds
3. Retirement account
4. Money market fund
5. Unsecured debt
6. Index fund
7. Mutual funds
8. Exchange traded funds
9. Securities
10. Diversification
11. Portfolio
12. Allocation
13. Target-based
14. Asset class
15. Outperform
16. Dividends
17. Corporate bond
18. Upgrade
19. Windfall
20. Triple-A rated bond
21. Default
22. Double-B rated bond
23. Blue-chip
24. Speculative
25. Nostrum
26. Panacea

Now let's listen in on a conversation about what you need to know when you're getting started with investments.

I'm not sure how I should start developing an **investment portfolio**. *Can you give me some beginner's advice?*

I'll do my best. I'll assume you have some **funds** already in a **retirement account** or a **money market fund**. I'll also assume you don't have any significant **unsecured debt**. If you're interested in long term investment planning, you could start by researching broad-based **index funds** in the form of **mutual funds** or **exchange traded funds**. Since you're just starting, it's best to stay away from individual **securities**. Those wouldn't let you create much **diversification** in your **portfolio** while you're learning the principles of investing. Index funds will give you diversification even if you only invest in one or two of them.

You could also look into a low-cost **allocation** portfolio, or a **target-based** portfolio that would give you representation from most of the major **asset classes**.

Thank you, that's very helpful. Do mutual funds tend to **outperform** *one another, or do they mostly provide the same annual* **dividends**?

Well, suppose a fund has invested in a **corporate bond** that unexpectedly receives an **upgrade**. That **windfall** could be reflected in better than average performance for the fund. The chance that a **Triple-A rated bond** would **default** in its first year is one in ten thousand. But for a **Double-B rated bond**, the chance is one in five hundred. That's a very significant difference. Sometimes performance can also be improved by adding more **blue-chip** securities, or by eliminating highly **speculative** stocks. "Buy low and sell high" is a reassuring **nostrum**, but it's hardly a **panacea** in the real world.

....

INVESTMENT PORTFOLIO

Definition: An investment portfolio is a pool of investments through which investors intend to diversify their holdings. The primary purpose of an investment portfolio, as opposed to heavily investing in one or two stocks, is to minimize risk. A typical portfolio will include stocks in high risk, moderate risk, and low risk categories.

Sentence Example: Sharon had some low-priced tech startups in her investment portfolio, and also a few shares of Google and Apple.

FUNDS

Definition: Funds is a word that usually refers to substantial amounts of money that are used for investments rather than for everyday purchases or the paying of bills. The word can also refer to the investment itself, such as a retirement fund or a mutual fund.

Sentence Example: Because his bank account was low on funds, Peter missed a major investment opportunity.

RETIREMENT ACCOUNT

Definition: A retirement account is a long-term financial investment that allows individuals to set aside money each year until their retirement, with taxes on the earnings deferred or eliminated. Retirement accounts can be established through banks, mutual fund, or the US government.

Sentence Example: Younger employees who are just starting their careers often delay funding their retirement accounts, thinking they have a long time before they'll need such a thing.

MONEY MARKET FUND

Definition: A money market fund invests in short term instruments such as Treasury bills, certificates of deposit, and commercial paper. The principle goal of money market funds is safety in exchange for modest dividends.

Sentence Example: Roberta knew she would never get rich through her money market fund, but she wouldn't go broke either.

UNSECURED DEBT

Definition: An unsecured debt is an obligation that is backed only by the reputation and creditworthiness of the debtor. It is not backed by any specific asset.

Sentence Example: A credit card is an example of unsecured debt, because no collateral is required to get one.

INDEX FUND

Definition: An index fund is a mutual fund that automatically mirrors the performance of a specific index, such as the S&P 500. Portfolio decisions are automatic and transactions are rare, so the fund's expenses tend to be low.

Sentence Example: Linda's index fund was pegged to the Dow average, so she did very well during the 1990s.

MUTUAL FUNDS

Definition: Mutual funds sell shares just as a company sells stock to the public. Mutual funds then pool the money from the sale of shares to make investments in stocks, bonds, and other instruments.

Sentence Example: Steve invested in a mutual fund that his dentist recommended.

EXCHANGE TRADED FUNDS

Definition: An exchange traded fund tracks an index but can be more actively traded like a stock. Exchange traded funds are traded on stock exchanges, so they can be bought and sold more quickly than many mutual funds.

Sentence Example: Bill had no idea what an exchange traded fund actually was, but he nodded knowingly when his date started talking about one.

SECURITIES

Definition: A security is investment instrument issued by a corporation, government, or other organization. The official definition by the Securities Exchange Act of 1934 reads, in part, "Any note, stock, treasury stock, bond, certificate of interest or of participation in any profit-sharing agreement."

Sentence Example: Nora invested in a wide variety of securities, and especially in companies named after animals.

DIVERSIFICATION

Definition: Diversification is a strategy intended to limit risk by combining a variety of investments. A diversified portfolio usually includes stocks, bonds, and real estate, which are unlikely to go up or down at the same time. If you lose ground in one investment, you don't want to lose in all.

Sentence Example: Jim knew that diversification was important, but he put all his money into Apple Computer in 1987.

PORTFOLIO

Definition: A portfolio is a collection of investments owned by an individual or organization. A portfolio normally includes stocks in individual businesses, bonds—which are investments in debt designed to earn interest—and mutual funds, various investments that are invested by professionals or by mirroring indexes.

Sentence Example: My portfolio doubled after my inheritance from my late uncle.

ALLOCATION

Definition: Allocation refers to the systematic and scheduled distribution of resources over various time periods, product categories, or investment categories.

Sentence Example: The allocation of Mr. Blake's funds was controlled by a sophisticated computer program.

TARGET BASED

Definition: Target-based is a portfolio strategy in which various asset classes are periodically rebalanced, in order to maintain the portfolio's original allocations.

Sentence Example: When oil stocks started going up and buy signals were triggered in Herb's portfolio, his target-based allocation mechanism also had to be activated.

ASSET CLASS

Definition: The major investment categories, such as stocks, bonds, funds, and real estate, are known as asset classes.

Sentence Example: I want to take a position in a variety of asset classes, but commodity futures are too risky for me.

OUTPERFORM

Definition: An investment or investment category outperforms another when it delivers a better return in a comparable period of time.

Sentence Example: During the early 1990s, Gardenburger outperformed almost every other stock on the NASDAQ exchange.

DIVIDENDS

Definition: A dividend is a share of a company's after-tax profit which is periodically distributed to its shareholders. Smaller companies usually distribute dividends at the end of a fiscal year, while larger publicly-held firms distribute every quarter. The amount and timing of the dividend is decided by the board of directors.

Sentence Example: Because profits were down this quarter, there was no distribution of dividends.

CORPORATE BOND

Definition: A bond is a legal promise to the purchaser of the bond to pay a specific sum of money on a certain date. A corporate bond is such a document issued by a company rather than the federal, state, or local government.

Sentence Example: Corporate bonds issued by the Walt Disney Company were illustrated with a picture of Mickey Mouse, which inspired confidence in the purchasers.

UPGRADE
Definition: Financial instruments such as bonds and mortgage loans are assigned ratings by a variety of agencies. An upgrade occurs when an instrument's rating is assigned to a higher category.
Sentence Example: The financial crisis was made possible in part by upgrades given to highly questionable sub-prime mortgages.

WINDFALL
Definition: A windfall is a completely unexpected financial gain or piece of good fortune. It's a stroke of luck that suddenly appears out of nowhere, like a leaf blown down by the wind.
Sentence Example: Winning the lottery is not really a windfall, because a ticket must be purchased first.

TRIPLE-A-RATED BOND
Definition: A triple-A rating is the highest rating that can be assigned to a bond by credit rating agencies. An issuer that is rated triple A has an exceptional degree of creditworthiness and can easily meet its financial commitments.
Sentence Example: The mutual fund bought only triple-A-rated bonds, because safety was the fund's most important feature.

DEFAULT

Definition: Default is the failure to fulfill an obligation as required by a legal agreement. Failure to meet the terms of a loan, for example, can be called a default.

Sentence Example: When Mr. Gray missed three consecutive monthly payments, his mortgage went into default.

DOUBLE-B-RATED BOND

Definition: A double-B-rated bond is a low quality investment grade instrument, offered by an issuer whose credit is highly questionable. A double-B-rated bond might also be called a junk bond.

Sentence Example: When the company's bonds received a double-B-rating, the shareholders demanded a change in management.

BLUE CHIP

Definition: Blue chip securities are those issued by large, prestigious, prosperous, and stable corporations. Blue chip firms have a solid record of earnings and dividend payments in over many years, along with long-term growth potential.

Sentence Example: The term "blue chip" comes from nineteenth century gambling houses, in which blue chips were of highest value.

SPECULATIVE

Definition: A speculative investment is a questionable proposition. The investor tries to see into the future, which is always risky.

Sentence Example: Horserace betting is highly speculative, unlike investing in stocks and bonds.

NOSTRUM
Definition: A solution to a problem that sounds better than it actually is. Nostrums seem simple, but they're also usually simple-minded.
Sentence Example: Sometimes investors rely on old nostrums rather than current and accurate data.

PANACEA
Definition: A panacea is a single solution to many or all problems. Genuine panaceas are extremely difficult to find.
Sentence Example: Lauren rarely used the word panacea, but she did speak of finding unicorns or the Holy Grail.

Banking and Finance
PART THREE
(DAY 3, DAY 22)

Not everyone is cut out for a career in the financial side of the business world, but everyone can at least understand what financiers are talking about. Some of the words in this chapter have origins and applications outside of banking, while others are more sharply focused on that area.

1. Diagnostic
2. Perspicacity
3. Acuity
4. Pecuniary
5. Propitious
6. Dead cat bounce
7. Holistic
8. Ascertain
9. Liabilities
10. Ballpark
11. Affluent
12. Diversify
13. Net worth
14. Broker
15. Churn
16. Commissions
17. Positions
18. Vig
19. Run-up
20. Subprime
21. Leverage
22. Instruments
23. Short
24. Robo-signing
25. Algorithmic Trading
26. Boiler rooms

Here's a conversation featuring some words you may never have heard before, but if you stay in business—especially on the financial side—you're sure to hear them again and again.

What skills are needed for success in the financial industry?
Well, there are actually quite a few of them. Ideally, you have the **diagnostic** talent of a physician, the **perspicacity** of a police detective, the **acuity** of a psychologist—and, needless to say, **pecuniary** intuition for recognizing **propitious** investments and their opposites. You know a **dead cat bounce** when you see one.

If you're providing advice for a retail client, it's best to take a **holistic** view. By **ascertaining** your client's investable assets and **liabilities**, you can derive a **ballpark** idea of the potential earning capacities.

Unfortunately, many **affluent** clients habitually switch their advisors as often as they **diversify** their investments. And many high **net worth** investors work with several bankers at one time.

If you're a **broker** as well as an advisor, it may be tempting to **churn** an account in order to generate **commissions**. But some clients want a lot of action, so they expect you to take **positions** and they're willing to pay the **vig**. In the **run-up** to the financial crisis of 2008, some investors eagerly put money into **subprime** mortgages and other highly **leveraged instruments**. Sometimes investment banks even **shorted** their own clients. People were **robo-signing algorithmic** trades and turning banks into **boiler rooms**.

....

DIAGNOSTIC

Definition: A diagnostic talent is a highly developed ability to identify or characterize something, usually an error or malfunction of some kind. Diagnostic is the adjective form of diagnosis, which generally refers to the identification of a disease.

Sentence Example: The financial manager's diagnostic abilities were tested by the business plan of the new company.

PERSPICACITY

Definition: Perspicacity denotes keen insight and intelligence. It's the ability to recognize subtle differences between similar objects or ideas.

Sentence Example: The professor complimented the student's perspicacity in his paper on Moby Dick.

ACUITY

Definition: Like perspicacity, acuity refers to keenness of sense, but unlike perspicacity it can denote physical abilities such as sight or hearing.

Sentence Example: Sara's visual acuity allowed her to see that the ant had a crumb of bread in its mouth.

PECUNIARY

Definition: Pecuniary is an adjective that refers to money or finance, sometimes in an ironic or negative manner.

Sentence Example: The venture capitalist suffered some pecuniary embarrassments at the end of the dot com boom.

PROPITIOUS
Definition: Propitious means favorable, or of an optimistic nature. It usually is applied to a future situation or event.
Sentence Example: Changing the date of the shareholders meeting was a propitious sign, in Mr. Potter's opinion.

DEAD CAT BOUNCE
Definition: An unsustainable short-term rally by an individual stock or a market index in a generally falling environment. Inexperienced investors can mistake a dead cat bounce for a legitimate turnaround.
Sentence Example: When Kellogg acquired Gardenburger, the meatless hamburger company, Gardenburger stock experienced a dead cat bounce.

HOLISTIC
Definition: A holistic outlook considers all the possible influences and elements of a situation, even if their importance is not obvious. It's the opposite of a narrow minded or reductionist perspective.
Sentence Example: Nancy's holistic analysis of the stock market included studying weather patterns in Asia.

ASCERTAIN
Definition: To ascertain means to make a correct and verifiable determination about something. It often refers to the elimination of doubt.
Sentence Example: Once Joe ascertained the nationality of the visitor, he made changes in that evening's menu.

LIABILITIES

Definition: In finance, liability refers to a debt or other legally enforceable obligation, such as the negative outcome of a lawsuit.

Sentence Example: The Company's liabilities far outweighed its assets, so Barbara wouldn't touch it with a ten-foot pole.

BALLPARK

Definition: In business slang, ballpark refers to the scale of a sum of money or a transaction. Ballpark means a general financial environment.

Sentence Example: When Robby asked about a ballpark figure for the purchase price, the real estate agent's face turned bright red.

AFFLUENT

Definition: Affluent means having an abundance of wealth. To say a person is affluent is a more discreet and cultivated way of saying the person is rich.

Sentence Example: The entrepreneur was not yet a billionaire, but he was definitely affluent by most people's standards.

DIVERSIFY

Definition: To diversify means to spread assets over a wide range of investments in order to sustain or increase earnings while maintaining the same level of risk.

Sentence Example: Michelle decided to diversify her investments rather than keep all her money in petroleum stocks.

NET WORTH

Definition: An individual's net worth is the positive or negative difference between that person's assets and liabilities. In a company, net worth refers to the sum of the issued share value, any retained earnings, and any capital gains.

Sentence Example: Charles liked to calculate the difference in his net worth from one day to the next.

BROKER

Definition: A broker is someone who serves as an agent or intermediary in business transactions or negotiations. Most brokers must be licensed by the state in finance, insurance, or real estate.

Sentence Example: Helen had absolute confidence in her stockbroker, whom she had known for almost forty years.

CHURN

Definition: In business slang, churning refers to a practice by unscrupulous brokers of urging clients to make useless and unnecessary trades.

Sentence Example: The broker was fired for churning accounts out of greed to get commissions.

COMMISSIONS

Definition: A commission is a mutually agreed upon or legally determined fee that is paid to an agent, broker, or salesperson for service in a transaction, such as a stock purchase or a real estate sale.

Sentence Example: Jim's earnings were entirely on a commission basis, so he needed to keep his clients active.

POSITIONS

Definition: A position is a financial commitment by an investor in any market, as expressed by amount of owned items or the amount of owed items.

Sentence Example: Heather's position in the commodities market varied as the price of pork bellies rose or fell.

VIG

Definition: Vig is a slang word that's short for vigorish, a Russian word meaning winnings. In financial transactions, vig can refer to the commission paid to a broker.

Sentence Example: By the time Edward paid the vig on his home sale, he barely had enough money for a vacation.

RUN-UP

Definition: The run-up is the period preceding a notable event. A run-up may be an intentional activity, or its existence may be apparent only in retrospect.

Sentence Example: The investor was disappointed that he hadn't noticed the obvious run-up to the boom in software stocks.

SUBPRIME

Definition: Subprime is a term referring to a loan arrangement for a borrower with a weak credit history. A subprime loan carries a high interest rate for the borrower, and a high risk of default for the lender.

Sentence Example: Subprime mortgage loans are now seen as a major cause of the financial crisis in 2008.

LEVERAGE

Definition: Leverage is the ability to take a position in a market in way that can multiply the outcome of the investment compared to the resources expended. This generally involves using borrowed capital, in expectation that the profits from the investment will be greater than the interest on the loan.

Sentence Example: Sally's position in the stock market was highly leveraged, so the actual worth of her holding was hard to determine.

INSTRUMENTS

Definition: In finance, an instrument is a legal document that expresses an enforceable agreement, obligation, or right. Documents pertaining to borrowing, lending, and investing are legal instruments.

Sentence Example: It took Bob almost an hour to sign and execute all the legal instruments that the lawyer put in front of him.

SHORT

Definition: Short selling is the sale of a security that is not owned by the seller, or that the seller has borrowed. Short selling expresses a belief that a security's price will decline. It's essentially a bet against a security or a market index.

Sentence Example: The Big Short is a film about investors who bet against the overheated housing market.

ROBO-SIGNING

Definition: Robo-signing is a slang term for the act of signing a legal instrument without actually reading or reviewing it. Robo-signing was a common practice with mortgages prior to the 2008 financial crisis.

Sentence Example: Tom robo-signed the documents because he needed to refinance his house before the end of the week.

ALGORITHMIC TRADING

Definition: Algorithmic trading is any automated investment system that utilizes an advanced mathematical model for making trading decisions. The decisions are often automatically made and executed by computers.

Sentence Example: The brokerage had an algorithmic trading system that kicked in whenever the Dow rose or fell substantially.

BOILER ROOM

Definition: In business slang, a boiler room is a brokerage firm that uses aggressive telephone sales tactics to sell low value, high risk securities. Generally the securities are nearly worthless penny stocks.

Sentence Example: In The Wolf of Wall Street, Leonardo DiCaprio plays the operator of a boiler room.

Banking and Finance
PART FOUR
(DAY 4, DAY 22)

Welcome to our fourth and final chapter on the vocabulary of banking and finance. Everyone knows about the bulls and bears of Wall Street, but there are many more financial metaphors, as well as technical words and phrases. This chapter introduces some of the most essential ones.

1. Bull
2. Bear
3. Investment product
4. Dow
5. Recession
6. Trough
7. Prescient
8. Hedge funds
9. Swaps
10. Arbitrage
11. Derivatives
12. Plain Vanilla
13. Private equity
14. Exotics
15. Structured products
16. Capitalization
17. Institutional investors
18. Pension funds
19. Beauty contest
20. Dog and Pony
21. Fire drill
22. Chinese fire drill
23. Sturm und Drang
24. IPO
25. Bake-off

Money may not be funny, but talking about it in an irreverent way can at least lighten the mood. Why a bake-off? What is a fire drill? Listen and learn from this dialogue between an experienced investor and someone who's newer to the game.

In general, is it better to be a **bull** *or a* **bear** *with most* **investment products**?

Well, over the long-term the **Dow** has risen, so long-term bulls have profited. But there have also been extended **recessions** and market **troughs** when bears have seemed **prescient**.

I suppose an investor can also be a **bull** *one day and a* **bear** *the next.*

Yes, and changes can happen very quickly. **Hedge funds** make that possible by aggressive use of **swaps**, **arbitrage**, and **derivatives**. But bulls and bears can participate in many ways, from **plain vanilla** stock purchases to **private equity**—although **exotics** and **structured products** require much higher **capitalization**.

I assume there's intense competition among banks for wealthy individuals and **institutional investors** *like* **pension funds**.

That's very true. When investment banks are in a **beauty contest**, they create elaborate **dog and ponies** for prospective clients. Sometimes when a big client appears unexpectedly, this can generate a **fire drill** or even a **Chinese fire drill**.

The ability of an employee to perform well under that kind of *sturm und drang* is a good predictor of success. If your supervisor suddenly announces that there's an **IPO bake-off** in the morning, you'd better have the capacity to work all night.

BULL
Definition: A bullish investor is one who is optimistic about the market and invests accordingly. Bulls like to point out that the over the long term markets have trended upwards. That belief allows them to ride out downturns and resist temptation to sell out of fear.
Sentence Example: Warren Buffett is the personification of a bull investor.

BEAR
Definition: Although markets have always risen eventually, short term or long term losing streaks can generate profits for bear investors, who bet that stocks will fall.
Sentence Example: The end of the dot com boom in the late 1990s started a bear market that lasted several years.

INVESTMENT PRODUCT
Definition: Within the financial industry, stocks, bonds, options, and other choices offered to the public are known as investment products.
Sentence Example: The Company provided a wide range of investment products to fit a variety of possible strategies.

DOW
Definition: The Dow Jones Industrial Average, often called the Dow, is the most watched stock market in the world.

The Dow includes companies like General Electric, Microsoft, Exxon, and Apple. The Dow Jones Company owns the Dow Jones Industrial Average as well as other indexes.

Sentence Example: Twenty years ago it was impossible to imagine that the Dow would reach fifteen thousand.

RECESSION

Definition: A recession is a significant decline in activity across an economy, including industrial production, employment, income, and wholesale or retail trade. The technical indicator of a recession is two consecutive quarters of economic decline.

Sentence Example: The financial crisis now called the Great Recession began in 2008.

TROUGH

Definition: A trough is a low point in a line graph of market activity. It represents a period of falling value for a market index or for an individual stock.

Sentence Example: Peaks and valleys or waves and troughs are two financial metaphors that mean the same thing.

PRESCIENT

Definition: Someone is said to be prescient when he or she seems to have the ability to correctly anticipate the future. Prescience is more a matter of intelligence than of a mystical power, which would be called clairvoyance.

Sentence Example: The old coach was remarkably prescient in predicting the winner of every Super Bowl since the Reagan administration.

HEDGE FUNDS

Definition: Hedge funds are alternative investments that use pooled funds in order to generate returns for their investors. Legally, hedge funds are most often set up as private investment limited partnerships that require a large initial minimum investment from participants.

Sentence Example: Some of the wealthiest individuals in finance are hedge fund managers.

SWAPS

Definition: A swap is a private contract through which two parties exchange financial instruments. Swaps don't trade on exchanges and ordinary investors don't usually engage in swaps.

Sentence Example: Swaps and the swap market are a mystery to most non-billionaires.

ARBITRAGE

Definition: Arbitrage means buying a security in one market while simultaneously selling it in another, and profiting from the temporary price difference. A good arbitrage opportunity can provide profit at no risk for the investor.

Sentence Example: If markets were absolutely efficient, there would be no arbitrage opportunities.

DERIVATIVES

Definition: A derivative is a security with a price that depends on or is derived from other underlying assets. Typical underlying assets are stocks, bonds, currencies, interest rates and market indexes.

Sentence Example: Trading in derivatives was too complex for Mr. Potter, so he stayed with unexciting investments.

PLAIN VANILLA
Definition: Plain vanilla is a slang term for basic conservative, low risk investing. Plain vanilla is not a criticism. It's just a description of a very fundamental strategy.
Sentence Example: Claire's plain vanilla approach was to buy one share of Johnson and Johnson stock every six months.

PRIVATE EQUITY
Definition: Private equity refers to sources of investment capital from high net worth individuals and institutions. This capital is then used for investment and gaining equity ownership in companies, with an expectation of turning a profit after several years.
Sentence Example: Gordon's private equity firm was named after Sherlock Holmes, the famous private eye.

EXOTICS
Definition: Exotics refers to complex investment vehicles and transactions, such as derivatives, swaps, and private equities.
Sentence Example: The elderly lady loved to make exotic bets in the stock market, which she could execute on her computer without getting off the couch.

STRUCTURED PRODUCTS
Definition: A type of investment specifically designed and customized to meet a particular investor's financial needs.

Structured products generally focus on varying the exposure to risky investments.

Sentence Example: A structured investment product gave Mr. Potter significant participation in fixed income markets.

CAPITALIZATION

Definition: A company's capitalization is the total market value of all of its outstanding shares. Capitalization is determined by multiplying the number of the company's shares outstanding by the current market price of one share. The capitalization of an individual might simply mean the amount of assets minus the amount of debt.

Sentence Example: Norman was rich, but he preferred to say he was well capitalized.

INSTITUTIONAL INVESTORS

Definition: Institutional investors are large and extremely well capitalized entities—such as pension funds or mutual funds—that take large positions in blue chip stocks or other opportunities.

Sentence Example: The new apartment building was funded by twenty million dollars from an institutional investor.

PENSION FUNDS

Definition: A pension is a fixed amount, other than wages, paid at regular intervals to a person or to the person's surviving dependents in consideration of past services, age, merit, poverty, injury or loss sustained. Pension Funds are

funds created and maintained, as by a corporation, to provide benefits under a pension plan; an investment product
into which members pay contributions in order to build up
a lump sum to provide an income in retirement.

Sentence Example: One of the benefits to becoming a
school teacher is the great pension fund you will have when
you retire.

BEAUTY CONTEST

Definition: In business slang, a beauty contest occurs when
two or more companies compete for a valuable client.
Beauty contests often occur between banks, advertising
agencies, and law firms.

Sentence Example: Kevin calculated the cost of the beauty
contest against the value of the prospective client.

DOG AND PONY

Definition: In business slang, a dog and pony show is the
physical manifestation of a beauty contest. In large companies, it can include the hiring of a well-known entertainment personality. The goal is to show the client that no
expense has been spared to win the client's business.

Sentence Example: The ad agency's dog and pony relied
too heavily on an Elvis imitator.

FIRE DRILL

Definition: In business slang, a fire drill is an emergency
situation in which a large amount of work needs to be done
in an impossibly short time.

Sentence Example: When the fire drill started in the marketing department, Marjorie knew she was in for a long night.

CHINESE FIRE DRILL
Definition: In business slang, a Chinese fire drill is a situation that becomes disorganized as a result of time pressure, ineffective leadership, or a combination of factors.
Sentence Example: The CEO burst into the conference room and shouted, "It looks like a Chinese fire drill in here!"

STURM UND DRANG
Definition: Sturm und Drang is a German phrase that literally translates as "storm and force." A figurative English translation could be "thunder and lightning," or "shock and awe."
Sentence Example: There was sturm und drang on the New York Stock Exchange when the Dow fell 500 points.

IPO
Definition: Companies exist as either private or public. An initial public offering, or IPO, is the first sale of stock by a company to the public at large. If the company has never before issued equity, this sale is known as an IPO.
Sentence Example: The tech firm's IPO raised two hundred million dollars in one day.

BAKE-OFF

Definition: In business slang, a bake-off is another term for the competition between two or more companies for an important client, or for any hotly contested situation such as the hiring of a top executive.

Sentence Example: Steve Jobs lost a bake-off to John Scully in the middle of his career, but Jobs ultimately had the last laugh.

Negotiation

PART ONE
(DAY 5, DAY 23)

It has been said that in business you don't get what you deserve, you get what you negotiate. If that's the case, the next four chapters are very important. They present the strategies, the tactics, and most importantly the language of negotiation in all its startling, creative insight and irreverence.

1. Unit cost
2. Agreeance
3. Disconnect
4. Feasible
5. Bedrock price
6. Full Metal Jacket
7. High-balling
8. Mister Toad
9. Baked in
10. Bespoke
11. Low-ball
12. Anticipointed
13. Chisel
14. Kink
15. Back-of-the-envelope
16. Bottom line it
17. Optics
18. Oxygen move
19. Mission critical
20. Move the goalposts
21. For my lungs
22. The juice isn't worth the squeeze
23. Break bread
24. De-horse
25. Triangulate
26. Shot-caller
27. Green pea
28. Tony Bagadonuts
29. Time pig
30. Path forward
31. Pig in a python
32. Laundering the lemon
33. Putting socks on an octopus

Here's a dialogue between two experienced negotiators trying to work out a deal. It's somewhat intense—but no pro-
fanity, because good negotiators never get angry, they just
get even. Or more than even if they possibly can.

We can supply you with 40,000 components per month for
two years at a unit cost of $4.35. Are we in **agreeance***?*
Hmmm. There seems to be some **disconnect**. We want
nearly a million components. For that quantity, the cost
you're talking about doesn't seem **feasible**. Is that your **bed-**
rock price, or is that **Full Metal Jacket**? It sounds like you're
high-balling me. I'm not **Mister Toad**.

We've **baked in** *the size of your order and we've actually*
reduced the unit price from what we normally ask. We feel
we're providing a truly **bespoke** *opportunity. What unit price*
were you thinking of?
Something around $3.50 per unit.

Well, if $4.35 per unit is high-ball, $3.40 per unit is defi-
nitely **low-ball***. At that price we would be losing money on*
every unit.
I'm really **anticipointed**. I'm not trying to **chisel** you but
this is a very unexpected **kink**. I was looking forward to
wrapping this up **back-of-the-envelope**. We have a quote
from one of your competitors at $3.53 per unit.

We can't match that. But If I were you, I would ask myself if
they're sacrificing the quality of the component for price. Do you
want best in breed, or do you just want to **bottom line** *it?*

The main thing I want, frankly, is for you to understand the **optics** of this deal. What's your **oxygen move**?

Well, if you were to increase your order to 50,000 components per months, then we could **mission critical** *the unit cost to $4.15.*

For 50,000 units per month we wouldn't expect to pay more than $3.85 per unit. Can you **move the goalposts**? Because this is **for my lungs**.

I don't think we can go that far. If it's under $4 per unit **the juice isn't worth the squeeze**.

All right, let's **break bread** at an even $4 per unit. I'm **de-horsed**.

Well, it sounds good. But I'll have to **triangulate** *with someone in accounting.*

Wait a minute. I thought you were the **shot-caller** but you're acting like a **green pea**. Now you want to bring in **Tony Bagadonuts** from accounting? That sounds like a real **time pig**.

I hope not. But I'm afraid it is the **path forward**.

The path forward? It looks like a **pig in a python** to me. It looks like **laundering the lemon**. We had a slam dunk and now you're **putting socks on an octopus**.

UNIT COST

Definition: What it costs a company to produce, warehouse, and market one unit of a particular product. If it takes $100,000 to produce and sell 1,000,000 transistors, the unit price is $10.

Sentence Example: There are almost no instances of the unit price going up when a production run increases rather than decreases.

AGREEANCE

Definition: To be in agreeance is to be in a state of agreement. There's dispute about whether this word is legitimate but dictionaries do use it as a synonym for agreement.

Sentence Example: General Dynamics and its former CEO found themselves in agreeance concerning the scope of his severance package.

DISCONNECT

Definition: A disconnect is a break in the connection or communication between two or more entities. It can also refer to a problem or inconsistency. As a verb, to disconnect is to sever or end a connection.

Sentence Example: Management was eager to resolve the disconnect between Marketing and Advertising so it could move ahead with its new sales policy.

FEASIBLE

Definition: A task is feasible when it can be done without expending more effort or energy than it's worth.

Sentence Example: The study concluded that the company's move to Georgia was feasible, but added that it should be undertaken in stages.

BEDROCK PRICE
Definition: Bedrock price is the lowest possible price a company can charge for a product or services.
Sentence Example: Management asked the vendor to lower its unit cost by doubling production but the vendor said this was its bedrock price no matter how large the production run.

FULL METAL JACKET
Definition: The list price for a product or service, with no discount.
Sentence Example: I only charged him ten dollars, but Full Metal Jacket was fifteen.

HIGH-BALLING
Definition: High-balling is quoting the highest possible price you believe a consumer would pay for a product. At times, it's deliberately quoting a price higher than any consumer would pay in order to leave yourself room to come down.
Sentence Example: Many salesmen use low-balling as a method of luring customers, but Joe felt high-balling was more effective since it allows the customer to feel they've won something when you finally come down.

MISTER TOAD

Definition: A buyer who falls irrationally in love with a product or service, regardless of price.

Sentence Example: When the customer saw the diamond pinky ring, he went full Mister Toad and paid ten thousand dollars.

BAKED IN

Definition: Something that's included in a contract or business deal, the way raisins might be baked into a Christmas pudding.

Sentence Example: Legal argued that the more the company baked into the contract, the less likely it would encounter disagreements down the road.

BESPOKE

Definition: Something is bespoke when it's made to order to meet the needs or demands of a particular person or company.

Sentence Example: Jack wore his bespoke suit to the national business conference and handed out his tailor's business card to everyone who complimented him on it.

LOW-BALL

Definition: To "low-ball" is to deliberately give a lower price for something than you intend to charge. The principle is to lure the customer in, then claim unforeseen circumstances compelled you to change the estimate.

Sentence Example: Harris liked to low-ball, and would often engage in debates with his high-balling peers as to which technique was more effective.

ANTICIPOINTED
Definition: Anticipointed describes the state of getting very excited while anticipating something only to be disappointed later on by its reality.
Sentence Example: Harris agreed with his fellow salesmen that low-balling often made for an anticipointed customer, but argued that it made him a customer in the first place.

CHISEL
Definition: To berate, badger, or try to wear down the other party in a negotiation.
Sentence Example: I chiseled the car salesman until he made the excuse of having to go to lunch.

KINK
Definition: A sudden negative development in a negotiation.
Sentence Example: A kink took place in the meeting when we saw the boss's Twitter feed.

BACK-OF-THE-ENVELOPE
Definition: Something done quickly and casually, as in jotting down calculations on the back of an envelope.
Sentence Example: Sure, back-of-the-envelope estimates are generally rough, but they save time by giving everyone a ball park idea of what's involved.

BOTTOM LINE IT

Definition: Basically, this means to summarize as quickly and efficiently as possible, as in, "What's the bottom line?"

Sentence Example: Once employees got used to Ralph's management style, they understood he usually expected them to bottom line it.

OPTICS

Definition: Optics is how something looks or appears on the surface, often as opposed to how it actually turns out to be if one digs deeper.

Sentence Example: In a fast-paced consumer society like ours, "optics" is often the first and last word in how a shopper responds to a product.

OXYGEN MOVE

Definition: Breathing new life into something; giving it an instant infusion of energy.

Sentence Example: Restyling the 2016 model was an oxygen move if ever there was one, the previous body style having grown as tired as white bread.

MISSION CRITICAL

Definition: An action which is vital to the success of a business or one of its operations, and whose failure will endanger that business.

Sentence Example: The new concession area is mission critical for stadium attendance, as fans have gotten tired of nothing but hotdogs and chips.

MOVE THE GOALPOSTS

Definition: Moving the goalposts means changing the terms or rules or parameters of a project while the project is in mid-stream.

Sentence Example: We thought we'd agreed on the terms of the contract until they moved the goalposts, and we found ourselves back at square one.

FOR MY LUNGS

Definition: A desperate measure taken in a dire situation.

Sentence Example: After losing half my net worth in the stock market, I bought ten thousand dollars of Apple for my lungs.

THE JUICE ISN'T WORTH THE SQUEEZE

Definition: This expression is used when the benefit of getting something isn't worth the trouble or sacrifice it would take to get it.

Sentence Example: At first, legal felt the corporation should sue, but in the end agreed that the juice wasn't worth the squeeze.

BREAK BREAD

Definition: Literally, this means to share a meal. In business, it can mean being in agreement or harmony with a partner, sharing profits with him or her, or having an amicable meeting to arrive at an agreeable conclusion.

Sentence Example: If you're free, we can break bread on this on Tuesday and move forward from there.

DE-HORSE

Definition: To be stuck somewhere, as if you've fallen off your horse.

Sentence Example: The student became de-horsed when asked to spell chamois in the spelling bee.

TRIANGULATE

Definition: To triangulate is to introduce a third party or element into an equation that initially had two parties.

Sentence Example: Administration decided to triangulate with Human Resources before implementing Jim's recommendations.

SHOT-CALLER

Definition: A shot caller in business or corporate life is the person who makes those decisions which other people carry out.

Sentence Example: Generally speaking, you want one shot caller per division since decision by committee is unwieldy and can eat up valuable time.

GREEN PEA

Definition: An inexperienced person, especially in a business or negotiating situation.

Sentence Example: Some of Steve Jobs' green pea decisions turned out to be money-makers twenty years later.

TONY BAGADONUTS

Definition: Tony, or Joey, Bagadonuts is a generic name for no one in particular—in other words, for someone of little or no consequence.

Sentence Example: I went to the convention expecting big things from it but it was filled with Tony Bagadonutses.

TIME PIG
Definition: A project, and sometimes a person, that will consume or waste a great deal of time.
Sentence Example: This Instruction Manual is a time pig, but H.R. wants it, and Management wants it, so we have to write it.

PATH FORWARD
Definition: A dramatic way of saying the direction, or steps, a business needs to take to move on from here.
Sentence Example: Once R&D had resolved the problems with the self-directing antenna, the company's path forward became clear.

PIG IN A PYTHON
Definition: A tedious or slow moving process, metaphorically akin to a python digesting a pig.
Sentence Example: When Celia runs the meeting, it hums right along, but when Dave chairs it, it's a pig in a python.

LAUNDERING THE LEMON
Definition: Trying to make something look better than it is, or covering up for a mistake.
Sentence Example: The boy tried to launder the lemon by saying the dog ate his homework.

PUTTING SOCKS ON AN OCTOPUS

Definition: Putting socks on an octopus means attempting to do the impossible. Alternatively, it means creating needless complications.

Sentence Example: Sure, we can try to persuade our customers to upgrade their operating program every two months, but it's putting socks on an octopus.

Negotiation
PART TWO
(DAY 6, DAY 23)

Welcome to our second chapter on negotiation. Several of these words and phrases refer to foods and eating, three of them mention animals, and one invokes the heavenly after-life. Yet they are all about money and the art of negotiating for it. Here is the vocabulary for this chapter.

1. Message tuning
2. Settlement range
3. Least Acceptable Result
4. Maximum Supportable Position
5. BATNA
6. Clown walking
7. Bogey tactics
8. Surf and turf
9. Common goals
10. Concession pattern
11. Considered responses
12. Equity pie
13. Wasted work principle
14. Junior woodchuck
15. Fixed pie
16. Issue surprise
17. Padding
18. Pseudo-sacred issues
19. Squeaky wheels
20. Tying strings
21. Sinister attribution
22. Nibble
23. Quivering quill
24. "That's-not-all" technique
25. Play chicken
26. Heavenly approval approach
27. Prisoner's Dilemma
28. Leaving a little money on the table

The following dialogue concerns an important client about to be lost, and how to keep him and his business. It's the kind of situation that occurs every day, and having the right terminology to talk about it can save money. You're about to learn the difference between the Least Acceptable Result and Maximum Supportable Position, so give this your full attention!

*We're going to need to do some **message tuning** on Mr. Green or we may lose the order.*

Message tuning? What's the **settlement range**?

*Our **Least Acceptable Result** is ten dollars per unit. Our **Maximum Supportable Position** is probably fourteen dollars.*

Well, I see ten dollars as our **BATNA**. Mr. Green will have to take it or leave it. No **clown walking**.

*Sometimes I feel like he's using **Bogey tactics**. He acts friendly but won't commit to a deal. He wants **surf and turf**.*

Are there any **common goals**?

*Well, not exactly. Mr. Green wants to save money and we want to make money. But I have tried to establish a **concession pattern**.*

Good. **Considered responses** are always useful. Make it seem like you're in great pain so you win more of the **equity pie**. Employ the **wasted work principle**. Ask for time to do **junior woodchuck**. Write down some calculations that only you can see.

*This is certainly a **fixed pie** situation.*

You can change that, or appear to change it, by introducing some **issue surprise**. I assume you're capable of **padding** with **pseudo-sacred issues, squeaky wheels**, and so forth.

*I'm familiar with those kinds of tactics but I'm not very comfortable with intimidation. I prefer **tying strings**. I'm definitely glad I've been able to meet face to face with Mr. Green. On the phone and in emails I could feel **sinister attribution** on both sides.*

Don't feel you have to get everything completely nailed down. Even when he's got the pen in his hand to sign, you can still **nibble**.

*Oh yes, the **quivering quill**!*

His quill might quiver too, of course. Then you can use the "**that's-not-all**" technique.

But sometimes that really is all.

Honestly, I've never seen that happen. When people say it's their last and final offer, it's really just a challenge to **play chicken**. It's just an attempt to get you agitated and impatient, like the **Heavenly Approval Approach**. Remind Mr. Green of the **Prisoner's Dilemma**. I'm sure he's familiar with it. And if worse comes to worse, **leaving a little money on the table** won't be the end of the world.

MESSAGE TUNING

Definition: Modifying a communication to suit the needs or expectations of specific recipients.

Sentence Example: Roberta told the interviewer that message tuning was different from being untruthful.

SETTLEMENT RANGE

Definition: The acceptable range for a deal to be concluded, somewhere between the parties' maximum and minimum expectations.

Sentence Example: Mr. Brown has made it clear that his settlement range lies between twelve and fifteen dollars per share.

LEAST ACCEPTABLE RESULT

Definition: The minimum outcome that is still acceptable to one of the parties in a negotiation.

Sentence Example: We negotiated for access to the company's Aspen ski lodge as part of our Least Acceptable Result.

MAXIMUM SUPPORTABLE POSITION

Definition: The highest point in a range of potential negotiated outcomes that is still realistic and practical.

Sentence Example: After three days of meeting we realized that the maximum supportable position could not exceed twelve million dollars, even if ten million was in the form of stock.

BATNA

Definition: The Best Alternative to a Negotiated Agreement is the fallback offer that creates a take-it-or-leave-it situation in a negotiation.

Sentence Example: We began packing up our documents when our BATNA was turned down.

CLOWN WALKING

Definition: Posturing or stalling in a negotiation.

Sentence Example: The driver began clown walking when the policeman asked to see his license and registration.

BOGEY TACTICS

Definition: Creating an informal, conversational atmosphere in a negotiation for tactical purposes.

Sentence Example: Jerome didn't go for the bogey tactics that get started while the negotiators broke for lunch.

SURF AND TURF

Definition: An act of greed, like wanting to have your cake and eat it too.

Sentence Example: We found a surf and turf hotel that had both an ice skating rink and a heated swimming pool.

COMMON GOALS

Definition: A shared adversary of a shared objective that can bring parties closer together in a negotiation. Common goals are an opportunity to agree about something.

Sentence Example: A common goal for Mr. Green and Ms. Gray was their shared desire to resist the hostile takeover.

CONCESSION PATTERN

Definition: Signals sent by parties in a negotiation concerning the hardness or softness of their respective positions.

Sentence Example: We gave in on a few minor points in order to communicate the kind of concession pattern the other side could expect from us.

CONSIDERED RESPONSES

Definition: The tactic of responding slowing and thoughtfully to a proposal in a negotiation.

Sentence Example: As a way of communicating a considered response, Mr. Black always silently counted to twelve before replying.

EQUITY PIE

Definition: The total amount of effort devoted to a negotiation by both parties. The party seen as making the greater effort owns a bigger piece of the equity pie.

Sentence Example: Our lawyer felt we owned most of the equity pie in the negotiation because we had not slept for two straight nights.

WASTED WORK PRINCIPLE

Definition: When a great deal of time and effort has been devoted to a negotiation, that time and effort becomes a motivating factor for agreement. If no agreement is reached, the effort has been wasted.

Sentence Example: After two weeks of sitting across the table from each other, the wasted work principle caused the negotiators to agree.

JUNIOR WOODCHUCK

Definition: Extensive research, a reference to Disney comics' all-inclusive Junior Woodchuck Encyclopedia

Sentence Example: I junior woodchucked for two weeks on the term paper, and I only got a B-plus.

FIXED PIE

Definition: A negotiation in which gain for one side requires loss for the other side.

Sentence Example: A fixed pie negotiation is also known as a zero sum game.

ISSUE SURPRISE

Definition: The introduction of an unexpected area of concern, often used as a tactic to slow down a negotiation.

Sentence Example: As peace negotiations were about to begin in 1972, the North Vietnamese suddenly made the shape of the table an issue surprise.

PADDING

Definition: Tactically inflating unimportant issues in a negotiation as if they were essential.

Sentence Example: Our favorite padding tactic was to insist on the use of gender-neutral personal pronouns.

PSEUDO-SACRED ISSUES

Definition: The insistence by one party, for strategic purposes, that certain unimportant issues are too important to discuss.

Sentence Example: We made Mr. Green's advanced age into a pseudo-sacred issue by constant references to his tennis game.

SQUEAKY WHEELS

Definition: Adopting a negative, demanding, hostile, or emotional style of negotiating, so that the other side will give in simply to avoid the unpleasantness.

Sentence Example: Squeaky wheels will sometimes win concessions in a negotiation when the other side can't stand it anymore.

TYING STRINGS

Definition: The tactic of making one part of a negotiation contingent upon another unrelated issue.

Sentence Example: The Senator agreed to vote for the voting rights bill provided an amendment was attached concerning duck hunting regulations.

SINISTER ATTRIBUTION

Definition: The tendency for people involved in a negotiation to automatically distrust the intentions of the other side.

Sentence Example: The chief financial officer attached a sinister attribution to any communication for the Internal Revenue Service.

NIBBLE

Definition: An unexpected request for a last small concession just before signing an agreement.

Sentence Example: We asked for a nibble of a hundred thousand dollars just as Mr. Johnson was reaching for his pen.

QUIVERING QUILL

Definition: The tactic of seeming to hesitate just before signing an agreement.

Sentence Example: I mastered the technique of the quivering quill in order to keep the other side guessing.

"THAT'S-NOT-ALL" TECHNIQUE

Definition: The tactic of adding an unexpected bonus to a deal in order to conclude a negotiation.

Sentence Example: We threw in free tote bags for everyone as a "that's-not-all" technique.

PLAY CHICKEN

Definition: A threatening negotiation tactic to test the resolve of the other side.

Sentence Example: Mr. Carter's exaggerated gesture of standing up from the table and putting on his overcoat was simple a way of playing chicken with the investigating committee.

HEAVENLY APPROVAL APPROACH

Definition: A stalling tactic historically used by Japanese negotiators in which a negotiation is delayed while the approval of the heavens is solicited.

Sentence Example: We cooled our heels by the hotel swimming pool while the Mitsubishi people sought heavenly approval in the meditation garden.

PRISONER'S DILEMMA

Definition: A principle from game theory in which the pursuit of individual self-interest leads to collective ruin.

Sentence Example: The Prisoner's Dilemma is an experiment in which participants learn to cooperate through a process of trial and error.

LEAVING A LITTLE MONEY ON THE TABLE

Definition: At the conclusion of a negotiation, realizing that a somewhat better outcome could have been attained. The recognition of missed opportunities.

Sentence Example: A negotiator's sense of leaving a little money on the table is similar to a shopper's experience of buyer's remorse.

Negotiation
PART THREE
(DAY 7, DAY 24)

Welcome to chapter three on the vocabulary of negotiation. The conversation in this chapter is another in which a problematic negotiation is dramatized. Perhaps more than any other, this chapter is all about non-technical, very colorful vocabulary. It's just for fun.

1. Aces in places
2. Unpack
3. Pre-think
4. Plugging the dyke
5. Pulse check
6. Hen party
7. Rolling the tortoise
8. Left-lane
9. Lipstick on a pig
10. Belt-and-suspenders
11. Let it drip
12. Eat the elephant one bite at a time
13. Project creep
14. Lay your silver on the table
15. Race without a finish line
16. Populate
17. Leave-behind
18. Biome
19. Anointed
20. Evangelize
21. Adhocracy
22. Bucketize
23. Direct reports
24. Rocket surgery
25. Boil the frog
26. Gazump
27. Give the dog a bone

In the following dialogue an executive and her supervisor discuss an ongoing negotiation with a woman named Ms. Gray, who wants to keep rolling the tortoise and needs to change her ways. But it's not rocket surgery, and there's even a gazump at the end.

Aces in places? *Are we ready to* **unpack**?

I think so. But what are we trying to accomplish in this conversation? Is this a **pre-think** before we try to advance the negotiation? Or are we **plugging the dyke**? I guess I'm a little disoriented.

I would call it more of a **pulse check** *than a* **hen party**, *because things are already pretty far along. How would you describe Ms. Gray as a negotiator?*

Her number one priority is **rolling the tortoise**. Ms. Gray wants to **left-lane** everything, which can be to our advantage because she hates long meetings. She'll put **lipstick on a pig** in order to get out the door. But as you know, I'm more **belt-and-suspenders**.

Well, if you seem to be slowing things down she'll probably start agreeing to anything. She'll want to let things rip, so you'll want to **let it drip**. *Apologize for asking her to pay attention but tell her we have* **to eat the elephant one bite at a time**.

If anything takes more than five minutes she starts complaining about **project creep**. She wants me to **lay all my silver on the table** even if she's not really ready to buy it. She keeps worrying about a **race without a finish line**.

Give her some forms to **populate**. *That can be your* **leave behind**.

In another **biome** she could probably be a good executive, but now she's just the **anointed** one.

Very few people can do more than one thing well. That's why I like to evangelize about **adhocracies** *where things are* **bucketized** *for all your* **direct reports**. *It's not* **rocket surgery**. *You just have to be organized and* **boil the frog**.

That's not what we're dealing with here, but I'll get it done.

I know you will. And will there be a **gazump** *for me?*

Of course. I'll always **give the dog a bone**.

....

ACES IN PLACES
Definition: A state of readiness on the part of everyone in a meeting.
Sentence Example: The board chairman expected aces in their places by nine o'clock on Monday morning.

UNPACK
Definition: To explain and explore a complex issue in detail.
Sentence Example: When Sandra unpacked her idea for the chief financial officer, he finally understood what she was talking about.

PRE-THINK
Definition: To discuss an idea or an issue with a small group before delivering it to a larger audience.

Sentence Example: Before the negotiation began, the executives met to pre-think their asking price.

PLUGGING THE DYKE

Definition: A temporary solution to a larger ongoing problem; a small initiative undertaken to prevent a major disaster; a small stopgap measure to prevent a big disaster.

Sentence Example: If we can plug the dyke about our stock price until the shareholders meeting, we can save ourselves a lot of bad publicity.

PULSE CHECK

Definition: A short meeting or other communication to discuss the current status of a project or negotiation.

Sentence Example: Terry was getting pulse checks every hour from her supervisor because the deadline was at four o'clock.

HEN PARTY

Definition: An undirected conversation with no time limit or set agenda, as in brainstorming.

Sentence Example: Thomas Watson, the founder of IBM, was fond of meetings but he detested hen parties.

ROLLING THE TORTOISE

Definition: To bring additional resources or energy into a slow-moving project.

Sentence Example: We brought in some temporary hires in order to roll the tortoise at Christmas time.

LEFT-LANE
Definition: To give top priority to a project; to make sure everything is moving as fast as possible.
Sentence Example: The CEO left-laned my counter-offer after all the other negotiators had criticized it.

LIPSTICK ON A PIG
Definition: An attempt to make a situation appear more favorable or attractive than it actually is.
Sentence Example: John's exuberance about the merger in the board of directors meeting was definitely putting lipstick on a pig.

BELT-AND-SUSPENDERS
Definition: An excessively cautious person or strategy.
Sentence Example: We took a belt-and-suspenders approach to the negotiation because we really didn't know whom we were dealing with.

LET IT DRIP
Definition: Finding an excuse to move ahead slowly in a negotiation, often as a stalling tactic.
Sentence Example: The sellers were in no hurry to close the deal, so they let it drip in hopes of getting a better offer.

EAT THE ELEPHANT ONE BITE AT A TIME
Definition: To undertake and complete a large task by breaking it down into a series of manageable steps.
Sentence Example: We transferred our entire inventory to our website by eating the elephant one bite at a time.

PROJECT CREEP

Definition: Continual small extensions of a deadline until the project loses momentum.

Sentence Example: Project creep sets in when the participants are distracted by their other responsibilities.

LAY YOUR SILVER ON THE TABLE

Definition: To frankly and fully describe the amount, products and terms of your demand or offer during a negotiation.

Sentence Example: Once they laid their silver on the table, we became much more interested in working something out.

RACE WITHOUT A FINISH LINE

Definition: Frantic effort without organization or a clearly defined goal.

Sentence Example: The secret project to design a new garage door opener turned into a race without a finish line.

POPULATE

Definition: To fill out a document, whether hard copy or online.

Sentence Example: Let's populate the website right away because we're starting to get visitors.

LEAVE-BEHIND

Definition: Documents or other materials given by one party to another at the close of a meeting.

Sentence Example: Our leave-behind included all our annual reports for the last five years.

BIOME
Definition: A sensitive environment or market that could change rapidly.
Sentence Example: We can't take on any more full-time hires in the current regulatory biome.

ANOINTED
Definition: An employee who has been selected by upper management as someone who seemingly can do no wrong.
Sentence Example: Bruce could get away with anything because he was the CEO's anointed junior executive.

EVANGELIZE
Definition: To promote or advocate with excessive enthusiasm and energy.
Sentence Example: The manager evangelized a bright future for the young employees in the mail room.

ADHOCRACY
Definition: A minimally structured business where teams are formed only when they are needed to address specific problems. From the Latin phrase ad hoc, meaning "for this."
Sentence Example: The film business is an adhocracy, in which a full staff is hired for each individual production.

BUCKETIZE
Definition: To organize information into manageable groups.
Sentence Example: We're all going to get very confused unless we bucketize the data.

DIRECT REPORT

Definition: A subordinate employee who is supervised by a specific manager.

Sentence Example: Ian had a small army of direct reports but he rarely had time to listen to them.

ROCKET SURGERY

Definition: A humorous combination of two clichés: rocket science and brain surgery.

Sentence Example: The R&D department was under such pressure that they treated the new project like rocket surgery.

BOILING THE FROG

Definition: A change that is accomplished so smoothly that it goes virtually unnoticed. The phrase comes from the factually incorrect belief that frogs will jump out of boiling water, but will remain in place if the water is heated slowly.

Sentence Example: Paul's handling of the price increase was a perfect example of boiling the frog.

GAZUMP

Definition: A sudden increase in the price of a negotiated agreement just before signing.

Sentence Example: The buyers were not surprised by the sellers' gazump and they were fully prepared to walk away.

GIVE THE DOG A BONE

Definition: To add a minor benefit to a deal in order to show good will or to gain favor.

Sentence Example: The new owner of the business gave the dog a bone by promising to cover the employees' cell phone costs.

Negotiation
PART FOUR
(DAY 8, DAY 24)

This final chapter on negotiation offers more sedate and serious vocabulary than the previous ones. The topic is contracts—what they are, what they are not, and what constitutes acceptance or rejection of a contract. Here are the words and phrases.

1. Formal acceptance
2. Comfort letters
3. Void
4. Covenants
5. Conditions
6. Breach of contract
7. Jurisdiction
8. Due diligence
9. Quid pro quo
10. Repudiation
11. Injunction
12. Arbitration
13. Express terms
14. Exclusion clauses
15. Exemption clauses
16. Restrictive covenants
17. Implied terms
18. Quorum
19. Manny, Moe, and Jack
20. Company seal
21. Misrepresentation
22. Trademark
23. De jure
24. De facto
25. Liability
26. Joint and several liability

Here's a dialogue between two members of the same firm concerning a pending contract. As you'll hear, this involves not only what is explicitly written in the contract, but also what is implied. After you listen to this, you may not know as much as a contract attorney, but you'll know why it's important to hire a good one.

If we agree to the contract via email, does that constitute a **formal acceptance***?*
No, those are just **comfort letters**. Nothing counts until the document is signed.

And after it's signed?
Then the only thing that could **void** the contract would be if the other side failed to observe one or more of the **covenants** and **conditions**. That would be **breach of contract**. How that would be handled would depend on the contract's **jurisdiction clause**.

So we're ready to sign?
I think so. The key elements leading up to a contract signing are **due diligence** and **quid pro quo**. We have both of those, right?

Yes, we do. I think we've covered everything. What would be our legal remedy if the contract were broken or **repudiated***?*
A lawsuit, ultimately. But if there were something ongoing, we could get an **injunction**.

I'm sure nothing like that will happen. In any case, the contract includes an **arbitration** *clause.*

Sometimes something can come up even as the contract is about to be signed. It's important not to ignore whatever it is. Even if there's just an oral agreement made at that point, it will still be binding under the category of **express terms**.

I can't think of anything right now that might come up.

What about **exclusion clauses**, **exemption clauses**, and **restrictive covenants**?

We've dealt with all that, either explicitly or via **implied terms**.

A **quorum** will have to be present at the time of the signing. Call **Manny, Moe, and Jack**. We'll also need the **company seal**.

Hmmm. The company seal. I haven't seen it for quite a while. Is that a legal requirement?

I don't think so, but it's a nice touch. It's another way of certifying against any **misrepresentation**.

What if I can't find it? What's actually on it?

I think there's a picture of an eagle or something, and maybe the company **trademark**. Its absence doesn't subject us to any *de jure* responsibility, but from a *de facto* perspective the company seal is important. I'm sure the other side will have their company seal. It's an affirmation of **joint and several liability**.

Well, I'll start looking for it.

I hope it didn't get thrown out.

FORMAL ACCEPTANCE
Definition: The unconditional agreement to an offer, which creates the contract. Before acceptance an offer can be withdrawn, but once acceptance takes place the contract is binding on both sides.
Sentence Example: Since the buyer met our asking price for the house, we didn't hesitate to signal our formal acceptance.

COMFORT LETTERS
Definition: Any documents issued to support an agreement which do not have any contractual standing. Comfort letters always state that they are not intended to be legally binding.
Sentence Example: The comfort letters from Acme Heating and Refrigeration had no more legal standing than an annual Christmas card.

VOID
Definition: A void contract is one that cannot be enforced at all. Contracts are void when one lacks the physical capacity to meet the terms of the agreement.
Sentence Example: Because of the earthquake in Los Angeles, the $200 million contract for the Playboy mansion became void.

COVENANTS
Definition: A promise within a contract assuring the performance or non-performance of a specified act.

Sentence Example: One of the merger's covenants specified that rap music would not be played in the mail room.

CONDITIONS
Definition: The major terms in a contract. Conditions are the foundation a contract and if one of them is broken, the contract has been breached.
Sentence Example: The first condition of Mr. Brown's contract stated that he would remain as CEO for the rest of his life.

BREACH OF CONTRACT
Definition: A failure by one party to a contract to uphold its obligations, which can lead to damages against that party.
Sentence Example: When the horse refused to jump over a fence on the movie set, the producers claimed breach of contract against the stunt man.

JURISDICTION
Definition: The country or state whose laws will govern the contract, and in which any legal action must take place.
Sentence Example: Louisiana and California have different legal codes than other jurisdictions.

DUE DILIGENCE
Definition: The formal process of investigating the background of a business prior to enacting a contract.
Sentence Example: Our due diligence revealed the fact that Mr. Gold had been born in Iceland.

QUID PRO QUO

Definition: In a contract each side must give some consideration to the other in the form of action or money. This consideration is referred to by the Latin phrase quid pro quo, meaning "this for that."

Sentence Example: I agreed not to exercise a right of access over the farmer's land in return for a quid pro quo of twenty-five dollars.

REPUDIATION

Definition: A party's refusal to comply with a contract constitutes a formal repudiation.

Sentence Example: The family's repudiation of the lease agreement was based on the landlord's failure to provide hot running water.

INJUNCTION

Definition: An injunction is an order by a court that prohibits some action from being taken which is against the terms of a contract.

Sentence Example: When truck drivers fell asleep in their parked trucks, the judge issued an injunction against the teamsters union.

ARBITRATION

Definition: The use of an independent third party to settle disputes, as a way of avoiding court appearances.

Sentence Example: Contracts generally include arbitration clauses in which the arbitrator is named in advance.

EXPRESS TERMS

Definition: The agreements that are specifically stated in the written contract or that are orally agreed upon even if no written contract is made.

Sentence Example: The court upheld the express terms of Mr. Silver's oral agreement with Ms. Gold.

EXCLUSION CLAUSES

Definition: Elements in a contract that are intended to protect one party from liability if a stated circumstance happens.

Sentence Example: The contractor's exclusion clause did not require him to work if a bear was sighted within a hundred years of the house.

EXEMPTION CLAUSES

Definition: Clauses in a contract that try to restrict the financial liability of the party that writes them. For example, they may set a limit on the amount of damages the party may have to pay if there is a failure of some part of the contract.

Sentence Example: The roofer only had to pay a thousand dollars to the homeowner because of the roofer's exemption clause.

RESTRICTIVE COVENANT

Definition: An agreement preventing the parties from working with competitors during the period of the contract or afterward.

Sentence Example: Brian's restrictive covenant prevented him from working for another marketing firm for five years after the sale of his company.

IMPLIED TERMS

Definition: Terms and clauses that are implied in a contract by law or custom, without actually being mentioned specifically.

Sentence Example: It was an implied term of our contract with the rancher that cattle would not be allowed in the parking lot.

QUORUM

Definition: The minimum number of people needed at a meeting for it to proceed.

Sentence Example: In our company, a quorum generally means ten people.

MANNY, MOE, AND JACK

Definition: Any group of inconsequential, unimportant people, similar to saying "the usual suspects."

Sentence Example: After the first few rounds of the pro football draft, what was left were Manny, Moe, and Jack.

COMPANY SEAL

Definition: An embossed hand-press indicating official approval by a company.

Sentence Example: Since 1989, companies may indicate agreement to a contract without the use of a company seal, provided there are at least two signatures by the company's directors.

MISREPRESENTATION

Definition: Misrepresentation occurs when one party to a contract makes a false statement that the other party relies on.

Sentence Example: Mr. Green's statement that he knew how to fly an airplane was definitely a misrepresentation.

TRADEMARK

Definition: A name or logo registered with the US Patent Office that is protected by law.

Sentence Example: The trademark of the University of Alabama is a charging elephant.

DE JURE

Definition: A Latin term meaning "according to law." This is a strict and narrow classification of behavior.

Sentence Example: George expected a de jure resolution of his accident on the freeway.

DE FACTO

Definition: A Latin term meaning "in fact" or "in practice." This is a looser description of behavior than "de jure."

Sentence Example: The mayor's wife was the de facto chief executive of the city.

LIABILITY

Definition: A person or business that is subject to a legal obligation.

Sentence Example: The ice skating rinks legal liability extended to people who fell down in the parking lot.

JOINT AND SEVERAL LIABILITY

Definition: Parties acting together in a contract partnership have shared responsibility. In addition to the partners being responsible together, each partner is also liable individually.

Sentence Example: Although the husband and wife were divorcing, each was responsible for the other's credit card debt under the doctrine of joint and several liability.

Marketing
PART ONE
(DAY 9, DAY 25)

Welcome to the first of four chapters on the vocabulary of marketing, which is a different discipline than sales. Marketing is strategic and Sales is tactical. Marketers certainly consider what goes on between a buyer and a seller, but that consideration often takes place from afar, with many more variables to be considered. A primary focus is on educating consumers before they physically encounter a product or service. That of course means advertising, and increasingly advertising is online. It's all very scientific now, as these words and the following dialogue suggest.

1. Potent
2. Content curation
3. Tactics
4. Implement
5. Weltanschauung
6. Enhancement
7. Target audience
8. Promoting
9. Sentimental
10. Analytical
11. Demographics
12. Hot buttons
13. KPI
14. Babysitter
15. "Be back"
16. CAC
17. LTV
18. Qualitative
19. Quantitative
20. Personal
21. Operational
22. Beholden
23. Account manager
24. Discovery meeting
25. Insouciance
26. Ingenuousness
27. SWOT matrix
28. PEST analysis

The following is a dialogue between two marketing professionals who have different approaches to their work. They don't ever reach a consensus, but they quite cordially agree to disagree.

*Having a **potent** marketing strategy is great. But it's not very useful without **content curation**. In other words, strategies have to link with tactics.*

I'm not sure I agree with the distinction you're making there. As a marketer, I want to make money. That's all the strategy I need. Everything I do is a tactic to **implement** that **weltanschauung**.

*Well, I need some sort of **enhancement** besides building my bank account. I think our **target audience** feels the same way. We want to offer low prices but that can't be all we're **promoting**. We have to market feelings as well as products.*

I understand. Your approach is **sentimental**. Mine is **analytical**.

*Is it sentimental to realize that different **demographics** have different **hot buttons**?*

Maybe not. Maybe we're looking at the same thing in different ways. You focus on emotion. I focus on **KPI**s. You're willing to take the time to turn a customer into a friend. Neither of us wants **babysitters**. Neither of us wants "**be backs**." For me, time is money. I worry about **CAC** and its ratio to **LTV**. You're **qualitative**. I'm **quantitative**. You're **personal**. I'm **operational**.

Yes, I suppose you're right. It seems strange that we're going to be **beholden** *to the same* **account manager.**

Well, I think this has been a good **discovery meeting** for us. **Insouciance** and **ingenuousness** have their place.

You mean everything doesn't have to be subject to a **SWOT matrix***?*
No, but a **PEST analysis** always helps.

....

POTENT

Definition: Potent means powerful. A potent administrator is capable of exerting power or influence, and a potent argument lays out a strong position.

Sentence Example: The CEO felt the new vice president for marketing would be a potent ally.

CONTENT CURATION

Definition: Content curation is the narrowing down, assembling and presenting of content relevant to a particular topic.

Sentence Example: Faced with an overwhelming amount of data, the staff decided content curation would be necessary to clarify their position.

TACTICS

Definition: Actions planned in advance to achieve a specific objective or confront a threat. Tactics are usually local while a strategy is general.

Sentence Example: The committee anticipated resistance from higher-ups and decided to use delaying tactics to buy time.

IMPLEMENT

Definition: To implement is to "put into action." Implementing a plan would mean you've taken it out of the development stage and put it into practice.

Sentence Example: The cafeteria staff agreed to implement the new menu which meant there would now be separate meals for vegetarians.

WELTANSCHAUUNG

Definition: A German word meaning world view, or philosophy of life. A food company might believe consumers will only become more health conscious. Its Weltanschauung would be, "The Future of Food is Green."

Sentence Example: If he could be said to have a Weltanschauung, it was that people will always act in their own best interest.

ENHANCEMENT

Definition: Enhancement is the act of increasing something's appearance or value. Upgrading a car's interior without raising its price would be an enhancement.

Sentence Example: The enhancement of the office environment led, not surprisingly, to an increase in productivity.

TARGET AUDIENCE

Definition: A particular group at which a product, or sales pitch, or advertising campaign is aimed—for example, women under thirty.

Sentence Example: It was easy to define the lipstick's target audience but harder to decide which medium to use to access it.

PROMOTING

Definition: Promoting something means to raise awareness of it in a positive way. Ad campaigns, for instance, are almost always promotions.

Sentence Example: Even though it was a dinner party, Ilene couldn't keep herself from promoting her company's new initiative.

SENTIMENTAL

Definition: You're being sentimental if you draw on emotions and feelings rather than logic and reason. In business, a sentimental decision might be one based on a past image or graphic rather than on present day tastes.

Sentence Example: Certain brands of baby food remain popular as new generations of parents have a sentimental attachment to those products from their own childhood.

ANALYTICAL

Definition: To be analytical is to base conclusions on logic and objective information rather than on impressions and feeling.

Sentence Example: Lars was famous for his analytical approach to sales, which made him impatient when people spoke about how they felt.

DEMOGRAPHICS

Definition: The statistical study of populations often used to identify markets or market trends. A demographic is a particular group defined, for example, by gender, or age, or geographical location.

Sentence Example: In an age of shifting populations, demographics help define what sort of campaigns may be effective.

HOT BUTTONS

Definition: Hot button usually refers to issues that are emotionally charged. Which bathroom transgendered people should use is a hot button issue.

Sentence Example: Davis decided it was best to stay away from hot button issues at the stockholders meeting.

KPIs

Definition: A KPI, or key performance indicator, is a quantifiable measurement of a company's performance over time. Examples of KPIs are sales, net revenue, customer loyalty.

Sentence Example: Steve Wozniak believed that KPIs were important to certain sectors of the computer business, but not necessarily to the creative side.

BABYSITTER

Definition: A co-signer or co-buyer on a contract for a customer with weak credit.

Sentence Example: As the newlyweds needed a babysitter, the bride's father stepped up as a co-signer on their apartment lease.

"BE BACK"

Definition: A prospective buyer who never actually makes a purchase.

Sentence Example: The "be back" was eventually refused admittance to the store by the exasperated salesperson.

CAC

Definition: CAC, Customer Acquisition Cost, is what it costs a business to acquire one additional customer. If CAC is higher than LTV, the customer's lifetime value, the business is in trouble.

Sentence Example: Marge took one look at the CAC and realized the measures she'd implemented had turned the company around.

LTV

Definition: Lifetime value is the amount of money a business will receive from a customer during his/her life as a customer. If an average customer spends $500 a year over the course of five years, his/her LTV is $2,500.

Sentence Example: Bruce was resistant to treating his customers as numbers but had to admit he learned a lot while calculating their LTV.

QUALITATIVE

Definition: Qualitative measurements assess things in terms of their value or appearance. If you like how an ad looks, you've made a qualitative judgment. A qualitative difference is one based on perception.

Sentence Example: One qualitative difference between the two companies was the care Gucci took in packaging its product.

QUANTITATIVE
Definition: Quantitative measurements are based on things that can be counted or calculated. If a company sells 400 units on Tuesday, and 800 on Wednesday, Wednesday is twice as productive as Tuesday.
Sentence Example: Biology almost always takes a quantitative approach to issues whereas sociology tends to be more qualitative.

PERSONAL
Definition: Personal is anything which relates to an individual's private thoughts, feelings, appearance, etc., as opposed to his/her professional judgments or opinions.
Sentence Example: In my personal opinion, opinions, as opposed to measurements, are almost always personal.

OPERATIONS
Definition: The process of converting resources and/or data into goods and services that provides value to customers. Operations are the steps that have to be taken to produce a product.
Sentence Example: We in operations are always hands on, whereas our advertising division may spend a great deal of time spit-balling.

BEHOLDEN

Definition: The sense or feeling of having an obligation to someone who has done you a service or given you a favor.

Sentence Example: The entire staff felt beholden to the boss after he gave them an unexpected Christmas bonus.

ACCOUNT MANAGER

Definition: An employee who performs the tasks necessary to managing existing customer accounts, and who often attempts to expand the same.

Sentence Example: The customer insisted on having a meeting with the account manager since the two already knew one another well.

DISCOVERY MEETING

Definition: A meeting held to explore issues surrounding a particular aspect of business, such as client needs, sales tactics, and the like.

Sentence Example: The discovery meeting was useful because it gave all those present a chance to air their views.

INSOUCIANCE

Definition: A charming honesty and worry-free style of communication.

Sentence Example: Insouciance is actually a French word whose literal meaning is freedom from care.

INGENUOUSNESS

Definition: Literally, this means childlike innocence, freedom from reserve or hidden agendas, completely honest no matter what.

Sentence Example: Everyone felt the HR manager's memo discussing her recent marital problems was a prime example of her ingenuousness.

SWOT MATRIX

Definition: SWOT is an acronym for Strengths, Weaknesses, Opportunities, and Threats. A SWOT Matrix analyzes these to arrive at an assessment of a company's performance and outlook.

Sentence Example: Jeff's increasing reliance on a SWOT Matrix led his employees to joke he must have invented it.

PEST ANALYSIS

Definition: PEST is an acronym for Political, Economic, Social, and Technological. A PEST Analysis gauges how these four external factors affect, or will affect, business at any given time.

Sentence Example: As conditions in Argentina began to change rapidly, the Inventory Department scheduled a PEST Analysis every week.

Marketing
PART TWO
(DAY 10, DAY 25)

Language should be flexible. It should be intelligent. It should also, even when the topic is business, be funny to some extent. Marketing jargon is probably the most creative and humorous type of business vernacular. Here are the words and phrases for this chapter.

1. List-buying
2. A and B test
3. Direct mail kit
4. Big data
5. Analytics
6. Actionable analytics
7. Hyperlocal
8. Gameification
9. Freemium
10. Growth hacking
11. Cold canvassing
12. Pipe smoker
13. Millennials
14. Advertisement
15. Content is king
16. Baby boomer
17. Re-purpose
18. Pain points
19. Munchkins
20. Click-bait
21. Thirty-somethings
22. User-generated content
23. Real-time engagement
24. Re-targeting
25. Mobile optimized
26. Snackable
27. Storyscape

What is gameification? What is a freemium? What is the role of munchkins in the marketing world? You're about to find out in this conversation between two people who are obviously very serious about their work.

*Marketing used to be nothing but **list-buying**, running an **A and B test**, and sending a **direct mail kit** to 20,000 people. Now we're in the era of **big data**. The era of **analytics**.*

Well, that sounds good. But analytics by themselves mean nothing. I want **actionable analytics**.

*You're absolutely right. That's why we've got a team working on **hyperlocal gameification**.*

Gameification? Does that involve **freemiums**? Let me tell you something. Nobody ever got rich by giving things away. Gameification sounds like **growth hacking** to me. It's old fashioned **cold canvassing**. You're just going to get a bunch of **pipe smokers**.

*To reach the **millennials** you've got to be comfortable with **advertainment**. The principle that content is **king** will always be true. But content for a **baby boomer** is different from content for someone born in 1995.*

But baby boomers are the largest demographic. There are seventy-five million baby-boomers.

*Well, there aren't quite that many anymore. And actually **millennials** are now the largest demographic. There are eighty million **millennials**.*

All right. Then we need to **re-purpose** our content for their **pain points**, because I'm not going to hire a bunch of **munchkins** to create **click-bait** for **thirty-somethings** to play online games.

*We will need some new content, but we can get **user-generated content** through **real-time engagement**. And a lot of our old content can be **re-targeted**, especially if it's **mobile optimized** and **snackable**. People won't remember that they saw an ad on their laptops if we **storyscape** it for them on their **smart-phones**.*

....

LIST-BUYING
Definition: Marketers may purchase lists of names and addresses, or email contacts of individuals who are likely to be receptive to a marketing campaign.
Sentence Example: No matter how clever your marketing might be, careful list buying is the most important element.

A AND B TEST
Definition: Marketers often evaluate two competing concepts by comparing their results against similar lists, or by comparing a new concept against one that has been consistently successful in the past.
Sentence Example: After running an A and B test among alumni, the university changed its mascot from a tiger to an anteater.

DIRECT MAIL KIT

Definition: A direct mail kit is a physical marketing envelope sent through the mail to a list of potential buyers. The kit includes promotional information about the product or service, and an order card.

Sentence Example: The difference between a direct mail kit and a junk mail package is a matter of terminology.

BIG DATA

Definition: Big data refers to the massive volume of unstructured information available to companies by electronic means. Finding ways to manage and use big data is a key marketing challenge.

Sentence Example: In his presentation, Mark projected a graph of big data onto a large screen.

ANALYTICS

Definition: The process and technologies that enable marketers to measure performance are known as analytics. Analytics can become overwhelming because of the vast amount of data that is now available and the many tools that exist to evaluate it.

Sentence Example: Our meetings relied heavily on analytics and people rarely shared their individual thoughts.

ACTIONABLE ANALYTICS

Definition: Beyond simply quantifying what's out there, actionable analytics provide information that can translate into practical and profitable activity.

Sentence Example: The ratio of the cost of a Super Bowl commercial to the number of people who would see it was an actionable analytic for the General Electric marketing team.

HYPERLOCAL

Definition: Hyperlocal refers to marketing that is sharply focused on audiences in specific locations, often by relying on GPS data.

Sentence Example: The hyperlocal marketing campaign targeted families within half a mile of a Trader Joe's store.

GAMEIFICATION

Definition: Gameification is tactic of integrating game-related elements into a marketing campaign, especially online. For example, users might earn discounts for a product or service by taking part in an online game or survey.

Sentence Example: Gameification can be effective, especially when a cash prize is included

FREEMIUM

Definition: A Freemium is a pricing tactic in which an audience is offered a product or service at no charge for a limited period of time, with a billed upgrade occurring later on.

Sentence Example: Amazon offers Amazon Prime service as a one month freemium.

GROWTH HACKING

Definition: Growth hacking is a strategy for poorly funded startups to gain a following through free outlets such as Facebook, Twitter, and YouTube.

Sentence Example: Our only choice for publicity was intense growth hacking with kitten videos.

COLD CANVASSING
Definition: A form of prospecting for any and all prospective buyers.
Sentence Example: If a cold canvas turns up two percent authentic buyers, that's a big success.

PIPE SMOKER
Definition: An unproductive contact that wastes everyone's time.
Sentence Example: The pipe smoker loitered in the Apple store playing games on the sample iPads.

MILLENNIALS
Definition: Millennials are members of the population boom that took place between the years 1980 and 2000. They are now the largest demographic group in the United States.
Sentence Examples: Millennials definitely make different food choices than previous generations, and they also tend to eat less.

ADVERTAINMENT
Definition: Advertainment is a marketing strategy that blurs the line between advertising and entertainment. It can include tactics like product placement in films and television.

Sentence Example: When the quarterback twice mentioned a specific brand of beer in the Super Bowl interview, George wondered if that was advertainment.

CONTENT IS KING

Definition: "Content is king" is a decades-old principle of marketing that asserts the importance of good copywriting and image selection over gimmicks and technological innovations.

Sentence Example: Jill started to laugh in the meeting when the marketing director said "content is king" for the one hundredth time.

BABY BOOMER

Definition: Baby boomers are members of the demographic born between 1946 and 1964. For many years they were the largest segment of American population, and their buying habits dominated the marketing industry.

Sentence Example: While the baby boomer told his granddaughter about the invention of the hula hoop, she soon fell asleep.

RE-PURPOSE

Definition: Re-purposing is the marketing practice of adapting content from one medium to another, or of re-introducing past content into the present.

Sentence Example: We re-purposed the print ad onto our website without changing anything except the year of the car.

PAIN POINTS

Definition: Pain points are the problems a marketing campaign promises to solve. It's an axiom that people are more motivated by relief from pain than by opportunity for pleasure.

Sentence Example: The impossibility of afternoon traffic in Los Angeles was a major pain point for commuters.

MUNCHKINS

Definition: Munchkins were "the little people" in the 1939 film Wizard of Oz. Today the word can refers to any large groups of anonymous workers.

Sentence Example: The day camp provided summer jobs for a hundred munchkins from the local high schools.

CLICK BAIT

Definition: Click baits are sensational online headlines whose sole purpose is to drive clicks. The actual content behind the click bait is always disappointing and uninteresting.

Sentence Example: The image of a dinosaur graduating from Harvard was pure click bait.

THIRTY-SOMETHINGS

Definition: Thirty-somethings are an important consumer group often comprised of married couples with young children. They tend to be well-educated and seeking to balance their careers and parenting.

Sentence Example: The meeting at the new charter school overflowed with thirty-somethings.

USER-GENERATED CONTENT

Definition: User generated content is material submitted to a website or blog by its visitors. A high volume of user generated content can spare the need for new content to be written by the website's staff.

Sentence Example: User generated content is a basis of the next generation internet theory and practice known as Web 2.0.

REAL-TIME ENGAGEMENT

Definition: Real-time engagement is the amount of time an audience spends interacting with marketers through online games, chat chapters, or comments on blogs and websites. Real-time engagement can help a marketer to build interest and brand loyalty.

Sentence Example: The New York Times website offers real time engagement through an online crossword puzzle.

RE-TARGETING

Definition: Re-targeting is the tactic of showing a web user an ad that they've previously seen but that did not generate a purchase. Often an audience needs to see an ad several times before making a buying decision.

Sentence Example: We re-targeted our old list of homeowners in Florida because real estate prices are going up.

MOBILE OPTIMIZED

Definition: Marketing is mobile optimized when it's configured to be seen and used on smartphones, including online purchase capability.

Sentence Example: The Disneyland promotion was mobile optimized for both Apple and Android.

SNACKABLE

Definition: In marketing jargon, snackable refers to a short form web promotion that users encounter in a variety of internet setting and contexts. A snackable video, for example, should last less than a minute.

Sentence Example: Visitors to music sites have short attention spans, so ads definitely need to be snackable.

STORYSCAPE

Definition: Storyscaping an ad means creating a dramatic narrative context for the promotion, such as a historical setting or a sci-fi alternate world. It's an attempt to capture the viewer's interest with something other than price and benefits.

Sentence Example: We storyscaped the Mitsubishi spot with a background of pyramids and camels.

Marketing
PART THREE
(DAY 11, DAY 26)

This chapter is a total immersion in the sensibility of contemporary marketing, without benefit of translation. If some of these expressions already seem a bit shopworn—"low hanging fruit," for example—that only shows how fast this language can change, giving rise to acluistic, amazeballs, alpha geek, and fanbassador. It's supposed to be fun, but it's supposed to be serious too. As Danny DeVito once said, that's why they call it money. Here are the words and phrases.

1. The view from thirty thousand feet
2. Low hanging fruit
3. Second screen
4. Ideate
5. Land of the clay people
6. Acluistic
7. Grape
8. Etherized
9. Banners
10. Banner blindness
11. Wearable tech
12. Influencers
13. Amazeballs
14. Link rot
15. Vapor trails
16. CTAs
17. Bottom of the funnel
18. HTR
19. Friction
20. Mousetrap
21. Bird dog
22. Alpha geek
23. Fanbassador
24. Sidebar
25. Heterogeneity
26. Transparency
27. Evergreen content
28. Geofencing
29. Talismanic power
30. Swim lanes
31. Wantrapreneurs

The following is a dialogue between two marketers who are frustrated by trying to engage with today's online consumers. Are they angry or are they just hungry? At the end of the dialogue they decide to solve at least one of those problems.

*Let's start with the view from **thirty thousand feet**. The **low hanging fruit** are the **second screen** people. We need to **ideate** them as quickly as possible.*

But they're numb. I'm not saying they're dumb but they're definitely numb. They're in the **land of the clay people**. Totally **acluistic**. They've turned into **grapes**.

*Yes, they're **etherized** because they spend so much time looking at their screens that nothing affects them anymore.*

Remember when it was so important to have good **banners**? What you have now is total **banner blindness**. We've got to make the screens exciting again.

*That's easy to say, but maybe the screen is just a dead medium. Maybe the future is in wearables. **Wearable tech**.*

But there actually are opportunities for real **influencers**. We've got to think creatively. Have you looked at our site lately? It's **amazeballs**. There's **link rot**. There are **vapor trails** all over the place.

*Yes, I've looked at it and you're right. There are no real **CTAs**. Users aren't getting to the **bottom of the funnel** anymore and I don't blame them. I'm not talking about just the **HTRs**. I mean nobody. There's way too much **friction**.*

We've got to learn how to **mousetrap** people again. We've got to **bird dog**. Where's our **alpha geek**? A good **fanbassador** would also help.

*Um, excuse me. Just as a **sidebar**, fanbassadors cost money.* Maybe we can start by using our **heterogeneity** as a selling point—and also our **transparency**. We've got to be contemporary. We've got to be relevant. We wanted **evergreen content** but now the leaves have fallen off.

*We believed in **geofencing**. We thought our value proposition would have some sort of **talismanic power**. We've got to get out of our **swim lanes** and rethink all of that.* We can't put ourselves out there as the establishment. We've got to think and act like **wantrapreneurs** again.

You're right. Let's go to lunch! Like in the old days!

....

THE VIEW FROM THIRTY THOUSAND FEET

Definition: The View from Thirty Thousand Feet is "the big picture." It is when you look at the whole to see how the various parts fit together.

Sentence Example: Although he was normally a detail man, Jack recommended they step back and consider the view from thirty thousand feet.

LOW HANGING FRUIT

Definition: Targets and goals which are easy to achieve without a great deal of effort. Alternatively, it can mean an easy and receptive audience.

Sentence Example: After the business plan dispensed with repeat customers and other low hanging fruit, it moved on to the difficult area of increased productivity.

SECOND SCREENER

Definition: A second screener is a person who watches two screens at once, often a laptop and a cell phone, or two laptops, or two cell phones.

Sentence Example: It's hard enough to get the attention of someone who's looking at one cell phone. It's almost impossible if she's a second screener.

IDEATE

Definition: To have an idea, or to conceive of or imagine something. Ideate sometimes means transferring thoughts or desires to a third party.

Sentence Example: It was a popular cafeteria sport to watch Mark sit over his lunch and ideate.

LAND OF THE CLAY PEOPLE

Definition: An indifferent state of mind in which potential consumers are not reachable by marketing initiatives.

Sentence Example: Physically Jennifer was in Bloomingdales, but mentally she was in the land of the clay people.

ACLUISTIC

Definition: Without a clue, as in dazed and confused; a dimwitted person, whether temporarily or permanently.

Sentence Example: After getting hit in the head with a pitched ball, the first baseman was acluistic for several hours.

GRAPE

Definition: A completely passive individual.

Sentence Example: The grape was so spaced out that he didn't even react to the earthquake.

ETHERIZED

Definition: To be extremely inattentive, as if under an anesthetic.

Sentence Example: The students seemed to become etherized when the teacher explained long division.

BANNERS

Definition: A banner can be a basic unit of electronic advertising, often a large web ad featuring animated graphics; or it can be a graphic image giving the name and identity of a site.

Sentence Example: Given the increased number of downloads, Marketing felt the new banners were doing their job

BANNER BLINDNESS

Definition: Indifference to banner ads as a result of excessive exposure to them. It can also mean the tendency to ignore displays ads in favor of the content underneath them.

Sentence Example: Marketing argued that banners which stayed up more than two weeks resulted in severe cases of banner blindness.

WEARABLE TECH
Definition: Technological devices that can be worn by a consumer, such as Google Glass, the Apple Watch, or Oculus Rift. Computer devices that monitor exercise and medical conditions also fall in this category.
Sentence Example: If they invent much more wearable tech in the near future, Margot joked, I'm going to need three arms.

INFLUENCERS
Definition: Influencers are people who have the power to impact other people's purchasing and/or style decisions, especially in fashion and music.
Sentence Example: It would be difficult to over-estimate Jackie Kennedy or Michelle Obama as influencers of a certain class of woman. And the same goes for Taylor Swift.

AMAZEBALLS
Definition: Something startling and unexpected, either positively or negatively.
Sentence Example: When you ride in a Tesla all you can think about is how amazeballs it is.

LINK ROT
Definition: Link rot is the term applied to links on a website that are broken or out of date, or that point to sites which no longer exist.

Sentence Example: The new IT Team felt its first job should be to clear the site of link rot, since broken and unusable links always alienate consumers.

VAPOR TRAILS

Definition: Vapor trails are the legacy or residue of old marketing content on a website. They can be ads, addresses or links that are no longer relevant.

Sentence Example: After they'd cleared the company website of link rot, the IT Team got down to the business of ridding it of vapor trails.

CTAs

Definition: CTA, or Call to Action, are words that urge a viewer or listener to perform a desired function. "Call immediately," or "Buy now!" are examples of CTAs.

Sentence Example: You might not think a soft sell would be a good CTA, but viewers often respond positively to phrases like, "Why not pick up your phone and call?"

BOTTOM OF THE FUNNEL

Definition: Bottom of the funnel is the last stage of the buying process before the purchase is actually made. Alternatively, it can refer to where a buyer is in the buying process if he/she has made the purchase.

Sentence Example: It's every salesman's objective to get a potential customer to the bottom of the funnel.

HTR

Definition: HTR in business simply means Hard to Reach, as in a group or a demographic that is difficult to influence or access.

Sentence Example: Janice had considerable had experience with HTRs, but trekking to an Everest base-camp to demonstrate the new sleeping bag took the cake.

FRICTION

Definition: Friction is any element of a website that is confusing, distracting, or that causes users to give up and leave the page.

Sentence Example: The new programmers sought to make the website as friction free as possible, so that even the tech-phobic could navigate it.

MOUSETRAP

Definition: A mousetrap is a means of keeping users on a website; disabling the backspace would, for example be mousetrapping.

Sentence Example: You could say it was dirty pool to set mousetraps for web surfers, but that doesn't stop certain programmers from setting them.

BIRD DOG

Definition: To attract the attention of potential clients or customers.

Sentence Example: The new website design bird dogged six thousand users in the first twenty-four hours.

ALPHA GEEK

Definition: Someone well-versed and up to speed with the latest trends and information about all aspects of high technology and the online world.

Sentence Example: Instead of trying to be captain of the football team, the high school freshman aspired to the role of alpha geek.

FANBASSADOR

Definition: A fanbassador is someone, often an influencer, who advocates or markets for a particular brand.

Sentence Example: While the Kardashians are their own best fanbassadors, many others are ready to step into this role if the Kardashians will only let them.

SIDEBAR

Definition: A sidebar is a digression in a conversation, like saying "Excuse me." It can also be a public request for a private conversation.

Sentence Example: Julie, extremely tired of Rex's continual sidebars, requested a sidebar of her own.

HETEROGENEITY

Definition: Heterogeneity essentially means diversity, not just in people, but in plants, or any other grouping. If a collection of plants comes from many different geographical climates, they would be called heterogeneous.

Sentence Example: The advertising department insisted on heterogeneity in their new TV campaign as they wanted as many ethnic groups as possible to be represented.

TRANSPARENCY

Definition: Transparency in a company or political group is honesty and clarity in information given to the public. A group that is transparent does not engage in deception and lacks a hidden agenda.

Sentence Example: It is safe to imagine that after the diesel fuel fiasco, the government will demand complete transparency from Volkswagen.

EVERGREEN CONTENT

Definition: Evergreen content is content that never goes out of date; on the contrary, unlike popular music or newspaper articles, it always remains relevant.

Sentence Example: While anything relating to automobile safety in general is evergreen content, specific content changes with each new generation of cars.

GEOFENCING

Definition: Geofencing is drawing a virtual boundary around a real geographical area, usually to send a message. Say a smart phone user enters a particular area; a computer program will automatically send the user's smart phone a message.

Sentence Example: Lunch at Dave's Diner drew in 26% more customers once Dave began to employ geofencing.

TALISMANIC POWER

Definition: The almost magical ability of a marketing tool or technique to erase consumer resistance and sometimes, to even be adopted by the consumers themselves.

Sentence Example: The art director and composer hoped the jingle would stick in the minds of their customers and acquire talismanic power once they began to hum along with it.

SWIM LANES

Definition: In business, a swim lane is a person's specific area of responsibility inside the company or corporation.

Sentence Example: Once members of HR were invited to sit in on evaluations, they had a difficult time keeping to their swim lanes.

WANTRAPRENEURS

Definition: A wantrapreneur is a start-up business person with more enthusiasm than knowledge or experience. The "want" part of wantrapreneur comes from wannabe.

Sentence Example: The Mentor Group's mission statement was to help wantrapreneurs get their feet on the ground and guide them through the first difficult months of running a business.

Marketing
PART FOUR
(DAY 12, DAY 26)

This final marketing chapter introduces vocabulary with technical aspects yet there's a predictably irreverent and sarcastic attitude. The difference between impressions and conversions is important to know, as is the difference between pop-ups and pop-unders, or frequency and frequency caps. But it's all in fun, until you have to deal with a bunch of eye-ballers. To find out what that means, keep reading.

1. Pop-up
2. CTR
3. Pop-under
4. Serve
5. Impressions
6. Conversion
7. Frequency
8. Frequency capping
9. Bounce rate
10. Cookies
11. Market spoiler
12. Real-time bidding
13. Affiliate marketing
14. Deuce
15. Nickel
16. Candy store
17. Walled garden
18. Reach
19. Atmospherics
20. Brand promise
21. Eye-baller
22. Closing the loop
23. Barometric price leadership
24. View through
25. Advergames
26. Ambush marketing
27. Keyword
28. Paid search

In the following dialogue a veteran marketing professional speaks to someone with less experience. The wisdom—or is it weariness—of age meets the enthusiasm of youth. But in the era of high technology, ancient history is only twenty years ago. The gentleman in this dialogue speaks of affiliate marketing as if it were something from Jurassic Park.

I have no faith in **pop-ups**. *People really dislike them. The* **CTR** *for pop-ups must be close to zero.*

How do you feel about **pop-unders?**

Those are even worse! We could serve two hundred thousand **impressions** *and I would be surprised if we'd get fifty* **conversions** *from pop-unders. Of course, we could never reach that* **frequency** *anyway, because of* **frequency capping**.

But there are still some good things about pop-unders. If you've got a site with a high **bounce rate**, people will see your pop-unders very quickly because they're trying to get away from the site. And you've transferred some **cookies**. Our real enemies are **market spoilers**.

Well, I guess that's true.

You can also make some money with **real-time bidding**.

I'm just too old fashioned for all that. **Affiliate marketing** *is about as sophisticated as I can get. Who cares if it costs a deuce or even a nickel per click through? I still want a website to be like a* **candy store**, *a* **walled garden** *with* **reach** *coming from* **atmospherics** *and* **brand promises** *and* **eye-ballers**. *I just want to* **close the loop**.

Well, **barometric price leadership** is really the same thing as **view through.** It's just the newer way of saying it.

Well, I'm happy with the old way.
What about **advergames**? What about **ambush marketing**?

*I have no idea what those are. I know what a **keyword** is. I know what **paid search** is. That's about as far as I can go.*

....

POP-UP
Definition: Pop-ups are windows programmed to open randomly when you visit a webpage and to cover the content of that webpage. They can usually be closed with a simple click.
Sentence Example: George enjoyed the Victoria's Secret pop-ups that invariably appeared whenever his wife Emily used his computer.

CTR—CLICKTHROUGH RATE
Definition: CTR is the ratio of users who click on a site's link relative to the site's total number of visitors. If one hundred people click on a link while five hundred visit, the CTR is 1 to 5.
Sentence Example: Everything we've done so far has borne fruit in a lower CTR. We were at 1 to 11, but with our new ad campaign, we're down to 1 to 6.

POP-UNDER

Definition: These are the same as pop-ups, except they appear under the content of a webpage and become apparent only after you've clicked out of your current browser chapter.

Sentence Example: Pop-ups, pop-unders—do advertisers and websites really think they are effective? They must, since they continue to be a fact of internet life.

SERVE

Definition: Specifically, the delivery of an ad from a web server to a device, such as an iPhone or computer, where the ads are displayed on a browser or an application.

Sentence Example: The new computer system enabled the company to double its serving capacity without straining its other programs.

IMPRESSIONS

Definition: Impressions are the number of times an ad has been served, regardless of whether the user has seen the ad or interacted with it in any way.

Sentence Example: Bill is a big believer in maximizing impressions. He's convinced the more ad content you throw at a buyer, the more likely he is to eventually pay attention.

CONVERSION

Definition: Also called conversion marketing, conversion is the process of turning site visitors into paying, or potentially paying, customers, either by getting them to buy, or to think about buying by signing up for a newsletter or periodic emails.

Sentence Example: Jim wondered whether a Super Bowl ad wouldn't result in wholesale conversion, as opposed to numerous small venue ads where conversion was steady but limited.

FREQUENCY

Definition: Frequency is simply the number of times an ad is served to a consumer during a given period. For example, the same beer commercial could be served ten times during a basketball game.

Sentence Example: Are frequency and quality antagonists in advertising? Overexposure can undermine a good ad, but this same overexposure may make a consumer hum a jingle she'd otherwise ignore.

FREQUENCY CAPPING

Definition: Frequency capping means limiting the number of times one particular ad will be shown to a customer during a specific time period.

Sentence Example: There's often a fine line between frequency and frequency capping. You have to know when to stop, but you also have to know when to keep going. Good frequency cappers can walk that line.

BOUNCE RATE

Definition: This is the percentage of visitors who leave a site after viewing just one page of content. A "hard" bounce may be caused by a web address error, a "soft" bounce by a full mailbox. In general, bounce rate measures a website's effectiveness.

Sentence Example: Advertising was adamant that a 40 percent bounce rate meant that the company should reconfigure its web content.

COOKIES
Definition: A small electronic file that a website's computer places in a visitor's computer. Cookies track the user's movements on the website and remember his/her behavior and preferences.
Sentence Example: Some folks might see cookies as an invasion of privacy but cookies rarely contain personal information and often allow swifter website navigation.

MARKET SPOILER
Definition: An internet firm with a website that gives detailed comparisons of competing products and vendors so that consumers can make informed decisions free of the influence of brand identification, reputation, and so forth.
Sentence Example: Consumer Reports may have been the greatest market spoiler of the pre-internet age. And now that it's on the net, it reaches more potential buyers than ever.

REAL-TIME BIDDING—RTB
Definition: RTB refers to a system of real time auctions whereby bidders bid for on-line ad impressions. The bidding takes no more than the time required for a browser to load a page.
Sentence Example: A buyer has to be confident of his firm's ad needs to engage in a platform as quick and relentless as real-time bidding.

AFFILIATE MARKETING

Definition: In affiliate marketing, a company pays a commission to an external website which brings it business, either in the form of traffic, sales, new customers, or any combination of the three.

Sentence Example: Affiliate marketing brought in enough business to allow John to reduce his staff without suffering any loss in sales volume.

DEUCE

Definition: A two dollar figure, in whatever context it may come up.

Sentence Example: The old man bet a deuce on the longshot, and won sixty dollars.

NICKEL

Definition: Five dollars.

Sentence Example: We made a nickel on every hamburger, because we sold them for twelve dollars including fries.

CANDY STORE

Definition: A large inventory or elaborate display in a commercial setting, such as a store or a website.

Sentence Example: Amazon is by far the biggest candy store on the internet.

WALLED GARDEN

Definition: First, a software system where the carrier has complete control over applications and offers a restricted range of information to its subscribers. Kindle and Nook are examples. Second, a circumscribed environment designed to keep those within it sufficiently satisfied that they don't try to get out. Time Warner Cable, for instance. **Sentence Example:** Walled gardens by definition want to keep you inside them, since otherwise they wouldn't have walls, right?

REACH

Definition: The total number of people who see your message. Alternatively, the segment of a demographic or niche group you access at least once during an ad campaign.

Sentence Example: Employing diversity in their ad campaign broadened the company's reach, and gave it credibility with a new demographic.

ATMOSPHERICS

Definition: Environmental factors influence a consumer's mood. Retailers employ color, music, product arrangement, design and lighting, to name a few, to create a disposition that encourages shopping and, hopefully, buying.

Sentence Example: Ever since industrial psychologists pointed out the value of atmospherics, even big box stores have become conscious of their layout and design.

BRAND PROMISE

Definition: A brand promise is what the brand promises, in advertising or marketing campaigns, to deliver to its consumer. Sometimes a brand promise becomes an integral part of the brand, as with Ivory Snow.

Sentence Example: Ideally, over time, a brand will become so fixed in the public mind that its brand promise will no longer need explaining.

EYE-BALLER
Definition: Anything that attracts the attention of potential customers or clients, no matter how irrelevant it might seem.

Sentence Example: The life-size cutout of an elephant was as excellent eye-baller at the trade show.

CLOSING THE LOOP
Definition: Closing the loop is another way of saying closing the deal. In advertising, it means someone bought something because of an ad. Elsewhere, to close the loop is insure a system remains stable.

Sentence Example: Marketing insisted its salespeople pay special attention to closing the loop—and not assume that at some point momentum would take over and the sale would complete itself.

BAROMETRIC PRICE LEADERSHIP
Definition: This refers to a situation where one company establishes the product price point for its industry and other companies, generally smaller ones, follow suit.

Sentence Example: The internet has allowed smaller firms to challenge the barometric price leadership of commercial giants by appealing to niche markets.

VIEW THROUGH

Definition: View through measures consumers' behavior during a certain period after they've been served an ad. If the view through period is set to 30 days, the consumer's relevant actions during that time can be attributed to the ad.

Sentence Example: While Advertising felt the view through period should be longer, Marketing argued for a minimum view through since it's been proven consumers have short memories.

ADVERGAMES

Definition: An internet based video game that contains a plug for a product, service or company. Some advergames are marketing tools created by companies solely to promote one of their products.

Sentence Example: As a skilled marketer, Jack had to admire the advergame savvy that went into colorizing the coke can in *The Road*. It was the only bit of color in the entire film.

AMBUSH MARKETING

Definition: By using this tactic, a company attempts to associate its product with an event with which it has no official connection. An example might be a skywriter writing Buy Shell Motor Oil over an STP sponsored auto race.

Sentence Example: The freelancer who sold homemade candles just outside the farmer's market was happily guilty of ambush marketing.

KEYWORD

Definition: This is a word, or phrase, that narrows a database search. For example, the word Bali will key a particular search, Bali Beaches a more specific one, Kuta Beach the most specific of all.

Sentence Example: When a keyword is very popular on Google or Yahoo, it pays to buy a word or phrase with that keyword so that your ad will appear at the top of the search results.

PAID SEARCH

Definition: A paid search is one where a website owner pays a search engine to place it at or near the top of the results for a particular key/search word.

Sentence Example: Something to consider about paid searches is that they are often marked as such. This can have a negative impact on certain types of consumers.

Sales
PART ONE
(DAY 13, DAY 27)

Sales really is synonymous with business itself. Nothing happens unless somebody sells something. Given the importance of sales, it is not surprising that a rich vocabulary has grown up around the topic. The ambivalent relationship between buyer and seller demands words and expressions of all kinds, and it is no surprise that America's greatest modern play dealt explicitly with a salesman. It is also no surprise that the most famous line from Death of a Salesman is, "Attention must be paid."

1. ABC philosophy
2. Collaborative selling
3. Adoption process
4. AIDA
5. Buying process
6. Purchase funnel
7. Buyer Persona
8. Buying Criteria
9. Lead qualification
10. Lead
11. MOFU
12. BANT
13. Objections
14. Value proposition
15. Buying signal
16. Cross-selling
17. Up-selling
18. FAB
19. Package
20. Quotas
21. Closed-Won
22. Closed-Lost
23. Closed-Won Ratio
24. Customer retention
25. Hole in the bucket syndrome

The following conversation introduces some basic terminology of the selling process. Some of these terms have been circulating a long time and some are much newer, but they are all pointed toward the same objective—and avoiding the "hole in the bucket syndrome."

*I've heard of the **ABC philosophy** of sales. Does that make sense to you?*

ABC? You mean "always be closing"? I would think that really aggressive orientation would be out of date by this time.

Okay, what's something more up to date?

Well, another version of ABC is "always be connecting." It's just a softer terminology, like **collaborative selling**. It's similar to replacing the idea of a selling process with what's now called an **adoption process**.

Wow, that sounds downright maternal.

Yes, but the operative principles are still the same. Are you familiar with the sales acronym **AIDA**? Or the metaphor of the **buying process** called the **purchase funnel**?

I think I've heard of that idea, but I'm not familiar with the details.

Well, suppose you were to imagine your ideal potential buyer. Let's call that your **Buyer Persona**. Even that perfect customer will still need a certain amount of information in order to make a purchase. We can call that information the **Buying Criteria**. As a customer's need for buying criteria is satisfied, he or she moves further along through the purchase funnel.

But what if they opt out before they get through the funnel?
Well, that can happen, because you rarely encounter your ideal customer in real life. But you can cut the chances of losing a sale if you've done effective **lead qualification**.

*Is there a difference between a **lead** and a buyer, or just a customer?*
Yes. A lead is a person or a company who has shown some interest in a product or service. Qualified leads are already at the **MOFU** stage—the middle of the funnel —by the time you encounter them.

But they're not completely ready to buy?
No, and you still need to further qualify them using the acronym **BANT**, which was developed by IBM way back in the 1950s.

What do those letters stand for?
They stand for Budget, Authority, Need, and Timing. But even if those criteria are met, there will still be some **objections**, which are actually opportunities.

How can an objection be an opportunity?
An objection is a chance for you to lay out your **value proposition** in detail. When you do that correctly, you'll find that it can actually motivate a customer even more. The customer will start sending out **buying signals**. It opens up

possibilities for **cross-selling** and **up-selling**. Another acronym for what that includes is **FAB**, for features, advantages, and benefits. You can present the whole **package**.

*Do you believe **quotas** should be used to evaluate sales performance?*

Well, I think quota is another old-fashioned word. I like to think in terms of sales that are **Closed-Won**, when the buyer purchases the product or service—or **Closed-Lost**, when the buyer doesn't purchase. Then we can find the **Closed-Won Ratio**, which is the percentage of prospects who actually buy.

Any final thoughts?

Well, the most important part of the sales process comes after the purchase is made. That's **customer retention**. It costs six times more to get a new customer than to retain a current one. So a company's survival can really depend on retention. A company can spend a fortune and still lose more business than they gain because of poor retention. That's called the **hole in the bucket syndrome**, where money leaks out faster than it can be poured in.

....

ABC PHILOSOPHY

Definition: Always Be Closing is a strategy based on the premise that everything in the sales process should be in pursuit of closing a deal in the shortest possible time.

Sentence Example: The ABC strategy is exhausting for both the seller and the buyer.

COLLABORATION SELLING

Definition: A sales strategy that assumes shared interests on the part of the buyer and the seller. Once buyer and seller realize this, they can both benefit.

Sentence Example: Collaboration selling is more like a conversation than an argument.

ADOPTION PROCESS

Definition: The stages a potential buyer goes through, from learning about a new product or service to either becoming a loyal customer or rejecting it. This can take place regardless of whether the buyer makes an initial purchase.

Sentence Example: Although Ms. Richardson did not buy the car, the adoption process offered by the dealership led her to give the dealer several referrals.

AIDA

Definition: AIDA is sales acronym that stands for Awareness, Interest, Desire, and Action.

Sentence Example: After many years of selling engagement rings, I believed in the accuracy of the AIDA concept.

BUYING PROCESS

Definition: The stages potential buyers go through before making a buying decision.

Sentence Example: Only an inexperienced sales person will try to rush the buying process.

PURCHASE FUNNEL
Definition: The process through which customers travel from awareness to purchase.
Sentence Example: The purchase funnel is a useful metaphor that has stood the test of time.

BUYER PERSONA
Definition: An in-depth representation of a sales professional's ideal customer, based on data, behavior, demographics, motivation and goals.
Sentence Example: Harold's buyer persona was a combination of many customers he had met over the years.

BUYING CRITERIA
Definition: The sum of all the information a customer wants and needs in order to make a buying decision.
Sentence Example: Referrals on Yelp were a key buying criteria in Mr. White's selection of a chiropractor.

LEAD QUALIFICATION
Definition: The process of determining whether a new customer has characteristics that justify a belief that he or she will make a purchase.
Sentence Example: The main lead qualification of the newlywed couple was their excellent credit rating.

LEAD
Definition: Someone who has shown interest in a product or service, often online.

Sentence Example: The man from Chicago was a solid lead who had qualified for a discount on the company's website.

MOFU

Definition: The middle of the funnel is the stage of the sales process in which a lead begins to voice questions and objections.

Sentence Example: When the buyer asked about the noise level of the washer-dryer combination, I knew he was in the middle of the funnel.

BANT

Definition: A sales acronym for assessing the qualifications of a lead. The letters stand for Budget, Authority, Need, and Timeline.

Sentence Example: The young man had three out of four BANT qualifications, but he didn't have the budget to buy a speedboat.

OBJECTIONS

Definition: A buying prospect's challenges and questions regarding the benefits of a product or service. A sale is unlikely to be completed unless all the objections are revealed.

Sentence Example: High price is an extremely common objection, and one of the easiest to refute.

VALUE PROPOSITION

Definition: A full range of benefits from a product or service that differentiate it from competitors.

Sentence Example: The value proposition of the cruise to Alaska included whale watching and an onboard casino.

BUYING SIGNAL
Definition: Any indication from a prospect which indicates that he or she is engaging with the practical aspects of the buying process. The most common buying signal is asking about price.
Sentence Example: The salesperson always mentioned free shipping as soon as buying signals began to emerge.

CROSS-SELLING
Definition: The process of selling ancillary products after the main purchase has been secured.
Sentence Example: A protective case for a newly purchased cell phone is a very common cross-sell.

UP-SELLING
Definition: The opportunity to sell a customer a higher-end version of a product or service.
Sentence Example: Up-selling business class tickets is very easy now that planes are always crowded.

FAB
Definition: Features, advantages, and benefits. A presentation that links a product's description, its advantage over similar products, and the benefits derived by a customer from using it.
Sentence Example: The car had so many features, advantages, and benefits that it literally sold itself.

PACKAGE

Definition: The full and comprehensive offer for a product or service.

Sentence Example: Low price is only one part of a sales package, and not the most important one.

QUOTAS

Definition: A quota is a set goal that a sales rep is expected to meet over a given time frame, usually a month or a quarter.

Sentence Example: The monthly quota was kept low so that the sales force would not become discouraged.

CLOSED-WON

Definition: A sales encounter that ends with the buyer making a purchase.

Sentence Example: The new hire's first customer at the Apple store was a closed-won.

CLOSED-LOST

Definition: A sales encounter in which the buyer does not purchase the product or service.

Sentence Example: Spending an hour with a customer is disappointing when it ends in a closed-lost.

CLOSED-WON RATIO

Definition: A salesperson's percentage of total encounters that conclude with a purchase.

Sentence Example: My generous bonus was based on my excellent closed-won ratio.

CUSTOMER RETENTION

Definition: A company's ability to gain repeat business from satisfied customers.

Sentence Example: The industrial supply company had such good retention that some customers were second and third generation.

HOLE IN THE BUCKET SYNDROME

Definition: Any business situation that generates more expenses than returns.

Sentence Example: My months of effort to land the big client were nothing but an example of hole in the bucket syndrome.

Sales

PART TWO
(DAY 14, DAY 27)

This chapter combines technical vocabulary with more colloquial words and phrases. It wouldn't be difficult to compile a full-size dictionary on the language of salesmanship, and this chapter is a good start.

1. Speech forcing
2. Bird in the hand moment
3. NSA
4. Data mining
5. Close encounter of the third kind
6. Demo
7. Demo goals
8. Demo ratios
9. Thermometer
10. Emotional sale
11. Intellectual sale
12. Who says so besides you process
13. Name floating
14. Name dropping
15. Triangulation
16. Tom Sawyer technique
17. Buyer's remorse
18. Borderlines
19. Buying warmth
20. Need behind the need
21. ELMO
22. Halftime pickup
23. Feel, felt, found
24. The three whys
25. Is now/Should be then

The following dialogue explores the nature of the face-to-face sales encounter. It is literally the beginning and the end of business, the two ends of the spectrum with everything else in between. This is what the dialogue poetically calls the bird in the hand moment—or is it just one person trying to get another person's money? Not that there's anything wrong with that, as George Costanza used to say.

In our society there are quite a few instances of what we call **speech forcing**. *Those are times when people are required to talk whether they want to or not—like testifying in a court, for instance. A sales situation, from the point of view of the seller, is a speech forcing situation. The seller wants and needs for the buyer to talk. But the buyer will usually hold back.*
That resistance is strongest at the beginning, don't you think?

That's right. I like to call the first encounter with a buyer the **bird in the hand moment**. *It's like a bird in the hand because if you hold to tightly you'll crush the bird, but if you don't hold tightly enough it will fly away.*
When do you consider that the sales process is in progress? When you first greet the customer, or first speak on the phone?

No, I don't think so. It's a long way from **NSAs** *and* **data mining** *to a* **close encounter of the third kind**, *which doesn't actually begin until price has been mentioned for the first time. I suppose you could say that you've been selling all* *along, but the nature of the contact changes when money has been brought up.*

Some people also call that the start of the **demo**.

*Right. There can be **demo goals** and **demo ratios**. And within the demo all kinds of things can go on. You use your **thermometer**. You can have an **emotional sale** but not an **intellectual sale**, or vice versa. There's the **who says so besides you process**, which can involve **name floating** or **name dropping**. Those are two very different things but they're both examples of **triangulation**.*

The **Tom Sawyer technique** is also an example of triangulation, isn't it?

And of course there will be objections.

Yes, but if you proceed correctly you won't have to confront the objections directly. They can go away by themselves and there will be no **buyer's remorse**. But you have to be sensitive to **borderlines** and **buying warmth**. You're always trying to find **the need behind the need**. Most important, you have to know when the buyer is sending you an **ELMO** signal.

*If you do get an **ELMO**, what are some ways you respond?*

The **halftime pickup** can be very effective, and so can **feel, felt, found**, or **the three whys**. I also like **Is now/Should be then**.

SPEECH FORCING

Definition: An interpersonal encounter in which the nature of the situation compels one party to talk, as in a courtroom or a business presentation.

Sentence Example: A police arrest is not an example of speech forcing, because citizens have the right to remain silent.

BIRD IN THE HAND MOMENT

Definition: The very first moments of a sales encounter.

Sentence Example: When the salesperson felt the bird in the hand moment had passed, she shared a humorous story with the customer.

NSA

Definition: Non-Sales-Related-Activities such as surfing the web for product information or checking email.

Sentence Example: Our NSAs included fantasy baseball games for an hour after lunch.

DATA MINING

Definition: Online research specifically devoted to finding leads or probable customers in a territory.

Sentence Example: LinkedIn was the primary data mining tool for Tom's executive recruiting work.

CLOSE ENCOUNTER OF THE THIRD KIND

Definition: A salesperson's face to face meeting with a buyer.

Sentence Example: Compared to conversations on the phone, the buyer seemed completely different during a close encounter of the third kind.

DEMO

Definition: A fully developed sales presentation, including discussion of price.

Sentence Example: The demo did not really begin for an hour after the customer arrived in my office.

DEMO GOAL

Definition: The number of demos a salesperson intends to accomplish during a week or month.

Sentence Example: My demo goal for December is very different from my goal for August.

DEMO RATIO

Definition: The total number of contacts divided by the total number of demos.

Sentence Example: If I make 100 contacts and have 10 demos, my demo ratio is 10 percent.

THERMOMETER

Definition: A direct question to the buyer regarding the sales presentation such as, "Have I explained why so many people are purchasing these?"

Sentence Example: If Harlan had used his thermometer, he would have seen that the demo was off track.

EMOTIONAL SALE

Definition: The point in a demo in which a buyer feels very positively about the product or service being offered.

Sentence Example: The look in the customer's eyes told me that the emotional sale had been completed.

INTELLECTUAL SALE

Definition: The point in a demo where a buyer feels convinced but not excited about a product or service.

Sentence Example: The salesperson recognized an intellectual sale when the customer looked up from his calculator and smiled.

WHO SAYS SO BESIDES YOU PROCESS

Definition: The technique of building buyer enthusiasm by referencing other satisfied buyers.

Sentence Example: In the back of every buyer's mind is the question, "Who says so besides you?"

NAME FLOATING

Definition: Sharing names of people personally known to both the seller and the buyer in order to create credibility.

Sentence Example: I floated the name of the principal of the school that both my daughter and the buyer's son attended.

NAME DROPPING

Definition: Referencing names for bragging purposes that have no connection to the buyer or to the product or service.

Sentence Example: The salesperson dropped the name of Jerry Seinfeld, who had once walked past the store.

TRIANGULATION

Definition: The tactic of building interest in a buyer by referencing someone else's interest.

Sentence Example: The puppy's interest in eating her food was triangulated when another puppy began to eat it.

TOM SAWYER TECHNIQUE

Definition: Making an unpleasant chore seem like a privilege, from Mark Twain's novel *Tom Sawyer*.

Sentence Example: I made paying the higher price seem attractive by using the Tom Sawyer technique.

BUYER'S REMORSE

Definition: A customer's anxiety about a purchase after the purchase has been made, which may lead to a back-out or a cancellation.

Sentence Example: We often encounter buyer's remorse when a buyer's objections haven't been fully explored.

BORDERLINE

Definition: An imaginary line indicating where a buyer is on the path to completing a purchase.

Sentence Example: The prospect was so far above the borderline that she would have quickly signed the contract if asked to do so.

BUYING WARMTH

Definition: Non-verbal signs from a buyer that he or she is reacting positively to a presentation.

Sentence Example: The customer's smile was a sure indication of buying warmth, so the seller moved immediately to the close.

THE NEED BEHIND THE NEED

Definition: The hidden emotional motivation behind a buyer's explicitly practical interest in a product or service.

Sentence Example: Mr. Atkins seemed fixated on getting excellent gas mileage, but his need behind the need was to look good in the country club parking lot.

ELMO

Definition: An acronym for "Enough, let's move on," indicating a buyer's impatience with the sales process.

Sentence Example: The customer shot me an ELMO when I tried to demonstrate Microsoft Excel.

HALFTIME PICKUP

Definition: A salesperson's pretend ending to a demo without asking the customer for an order.

Sentence Example: The buyer looked shocked when I started a halftime pickup ten minutes into the demo.

FEEL, FELT, FOUND

Definition: A sales technique for dealing with objections based on three elements: "I understand how you feel," "Other customers have felt that way," "Many of them have found they feel better after making this purchase."

Sentence Example: Feel, felt, found is a very practical application for triangulating the sale.

THE THREE WHYS

Definition: Research has found that sales presentations are most effective when the seller asks "why" at least three times.

Sentence Example: The three whys technique flatters the prospect by showing sincere interest on the part of the salesperson.

IS NOW/SHOULD BE THEN

Definition: An understanding by the salesperson of how the customer feels now, and how the presentation should be crafted to bring the customer to where he or she needs to be.

Sentence Example: Success of the "Is now, should be then" technique depends on the seller's true belief in the product or service being offered.

Entrepreneurship
PART ONE
(DAY 15, DAY 28)

It was only recently—or at least only in the last one hundred years—that a large percentage of the American workforce found employment with large corporations. Before that, it was every man for himself—we see more of that coming back, which now includes every woman for herself. That can mean freedom and opportunity, especially if you have interest and expertise in the most dynamic areas of the economy. These words and the phrases, and the dialogue that follows, can get you started in that direction.

1. Entrepreneur
2. Sole proprietorship
3. Start-up financing
4. Intangible assets
5. Proof of concept
6. Copyright
7. Equity
8. Venture capitalist
9. Angel investor
10. Seed financing
11. Business plan
12. Business incubator
13. Limited partnership
14. Inventory
15. E-commerce
16. Outsource
17. Bridge financing
18. Liquidity
19. Breakeven point
20. Collateral
21. Corporation
22. Cash flow
23. Cash flow statement
24. Depreciation

The following conversation explores some of the issues around getting started as an entrepreneur—especially the legal issues involved with raising money. Fundraising may not be as exciting as inventing a better mousetrap, but you won't catch any mice without it.

*In an era when fewer people seem to stay with one company, or even one career, would you say **entrepreneurism** is the future?*
I wouldn't say it's the future for everyone, but being an entrepreneur definitely offers some big opportunities. Anyone with a laptop can set up a website and start a **sole proprietorship.** In all of human history, that's only been true for the last twenty years.

*I agree. But after you've got the website, if you really want to have a business you'll need some **start-up financing**.*
Of course. But **intangible assets** can make that happen without too much trouble. All you need is a **proof of concept** statement, maybe a **copyright**, and willingness to sell some **equity** in your company. If the idea is solid enough, people will listen.

*Which people are you talking about? **Venture capitalists**?*
No, that's not the first step. **Angel investors** are the first step to provide some **seed financing**.

*Wouldn't you need a **business plan**?*
I don't think a formal business plan is always necessary. In fact putting too much effort into that can seem old fashioned. I'm not sure what business plans look like right now

in Silicon Valley. If you've been working in a **business incubator**, that can provide some validation in itself.

So what happens after you find some angels?
You can set up a **limited partnership** and get to work. Now that you've got some capital, you can create **inventory**, whether it's physical inventory or something less tangible for **E-commerce**. You can **outsource** any help you might need. You may still need some **bridge financing** before you're ready to approach venture capitalists, but that's not unusual. Lots of startups find big investors before they have any real **liquidity** or get anywhere near the **breakeven point**.

Well, that all sounds great and we've all heard about billionaires who started by scrawling something on a paper napkin and got loans without any **collateral**. *But if I were talking to a prospective entrepreneur, I would still advise setting up a* **corporation** *before too long. And if there's not going to be a formal business plan, there still should be some* **cash flow** *and* **cash flow statements**.

I'm sure you're right about a lot of that. But there are people flying around in private jets who couldn't tell you what **depreciation** means if their lives depended on it.

....

ENTREPRENEUR
Definition: A person who organizes, operates, and assumes the risk for a business venture.
Sentence Example: At some point, every company was started by an entrepreneur.

SOLE PROPRIETORSHIP

Definition: A business form with one owner who is responsible for all of the firm's liabilities.

Sentence Example: Because it's a sole proprietorship, my company is me.

START-UP FINANCING

Definition: Funding provided to companies for use in product development and initial marketing.

Sentence Example: We needed start-up financing, so we called my rich uncle.

INTANGIBLE ASSETS

Definition: Properties of value that have no tangible physical presence, such as ideas.

Sentence Example: Mr. Black's sense of humor was his best intangible asset.

PROOF OF CONCEPT—POC

Definition: A demonstration or written document to verify an idea has potential for real-world application.

Sentence Example: My partner and I wrote up a proof of concept the night before we met with investors.

COPYRIGHT

Definition: A form of legal protection for published and unpublished literary, scientific, and artistic works that exist in some material form.

Sentence Example: In most cases, a copyright is much easier to attain than a patent.

EQUITY
Definition: An ownership interest in a business.
Sentence Example: I had to sell some equity in my startup in order to put gas in my car.

VENTURE CAPITALIST
Definition: A company that provides long-term capital funding to enterprises with a limited track record but with the expectation of substantial growth.
Sentence Example: eBay and PayPal received early funding from venture capitalists.

ANGEL INVESTORS
Definition: Individuals who are willing to invest and risk capital in startup companies.
Sentence Example: Stephanie met with an anonymous angel investor who wished to be known as the Monopoly Man.

SEED FINANCING
Definition: A relatively small amount of money provided for product development and market research.
Sentence Example: Seed financing for a rocket powered bicycle will be difficult to obtain.

BUSINESS PLAN
Definition: A formal statement of a new company's goals, the benefits of attaining the goals, and credible plans for reaching them.
Sentence Example: The consultant tried to explain the difference between a business plan and a prospectus.

BUSINESS INCUBATOR

Definition: A form of mentoring in which workspace, support services, and possibly some funding are provided to entrepreneurs.

Sentence Example: The Company called Y-Combinator is an excellent example of a business incubator, which *Fortune* called "a spawning ground for emerging tech giants."

LIMITED PARTNERSHIP

Definition: A business in which day-to-day operations are controlled by one or more general partners and funded by limited or silent partners

Sentence Example: In a limited partnership, the general partner is responsible for providing financial statements to the company's backers.

INVENTORY

Definition: The finished goods, works in process of manufacture, and raw materials owned by a company.

Sentence Example: A startup company needs to have at least enough inventory to fill its orders.

E-COMMERCE

Definition: The sale of products and services over the Internet.

Sentence Example: Amazon hugely expanded the universe of e-commerce.

OUTSOURCING

Definition: A company's strategy of using subcontractors or other businesses, rather than paid employees.

Sentence Example: We outsourced all our transcribing to a company in Mumbai.

BRIDGE FINANCING

Definition: A short-term cash infusion to a company that is expected to be repaid quickly.

Sentence Example: The online gaming company needed some bridge financing when its beta version kept crashing.

LIQUIDITY

Definition: The capacity of an asset to quickly be converted to cash.

Sentence Example: Real estate is a solid long term investment, but its liquidity is suspect.

BREAKEVEN POINT

Definition: The point at which a company's sales will cover but not exceed all of the company's costs.

Sentence Example: Many years passed before Amazon reached its breakeven point.

COLLATERAL

Definition: An asset pledged as security for a loan.

Sentence Example: As collateral for a loan, the entrepreneur offered his savings account as well as his pots and pans.

CORPORATION

Definition: A business that exists as a legally separate entity from its owners. Its important features include limited liability and easy transfer of ownership.

Sentence Example: On the advice of our attorney, our company changed from a limited partnership to a corporation.

CASH FLOW

Definition: The difference between the company's cash receipts and its payments in a given period.

Sentence Example: The investors were more interested in cash flow than after tax profits.

CASH FLOW STATEMENT

Definition: A summary of a company's cash flow over a period of time.

Sentence Example: The cash flow statement for July showed great improvement over May.

DEPRECIATION

Definition: The decrease in the value of assets over their expected life according to an accepted accounting method.

Sentence Example: The depreciation of our mainframe computer provided a significant tax advantage.

Entrepreneurship
PART TWO
(DAY 16, DAY 28)

These words and phrases focus on how to keep the spirit of innovation alive after the initial stage of an enterprise has passed. That does not necessarily happen by itself, so this chapter can be valuable if you want to keep the flame burning. Which you should, because there are plenty of people right behind you if you don't. Here are the words and phrases.

1. First movers
2. Late movers
3. Barriers to entry
4. Grand strategy
5. Functional strategies
6. Company culture
7. Company mission
8. Competitive position
9. Distinctive competence
10. Competitive reactions
11. Benchmarking
12. Leapfrogging
13. Mature industry
14. Cost advantage
15. Sustainable competitive advantage
16. Macro-environment
17. Differentiation strategies
18. Distribution channel
19. Matrix organization
20. Portfolio approach
21. Strategic business clusters
22. Value chain
23. Strategic alliances
24. Horizontal integration
25. Concentric diversification

The following is a dialogue between an aspiring entrepreneur and someone with more experience—a venture capitalist, perhaps. Where should a startup go after it's outgrown the basement—and especially if it's outgrown the garage?

Let's talk about how a company can retain an entrepreneurial spirit and identity after it's moved out of the garage or the basement. What are the issues for a company that wants to feel entrepreneurial even when it's become a corporation?

Well, there are two categories of companies that are making that transition. We call them **first movers** and **late movers**. Each of them faces different **barriers to entry**. And each needs both a **grand strategy** and **functional strategies**.

How are those strategies determined?

That depends on the **company culture** and the **company mission**. A company has to stake out a **competitive position** based on its **distinctive competence**. Then there will be **competitive reactions** from other companies in the field, which will help the firm define its own strategies.

*I suppose **benchmarking** is an important part of all that.*

Yes, it is. Sometimes companies are able to **leapfrog** into a very advantageous position, which is of course a good outcome. That's often possible when entering **mature industries**.

As an entrepreneurial company continues to grow, what are some of the steps?

Established firms often have a **cost advantage** that's difficult for newcomers to beat. That's what's called a **sustainable competitive advantage.** So a new company has to look at the **macro-environment** and evolve its own **differentiation strategies** and **distribution channels.**

What could some of those be?

Some of them can be purely organizational. A company can develop a **matrix organization**, or it could follow a **portfolio approach**, both of which are different from traditional **strategic business clusters.** The goal is to create an efficient and productive **value chain.** Beyond that, growing companies can initiate **strategic alliances, horizontal integration,** and **concentric diversification.** But those are just buzzwords for the same principle, which is you either eat or get eaten.

....

FIRST MOVERS
Definition: Firms entering new markets or developing new products before other firms.
Sentence Example: It's not clear whether the Wright Brothers were the first movers in the airplane industry, but they were certainly close.

LATE MOVERS
Definition: Firms entering new markets or developing new products after they have been established by other firms.
Sentence Example: If Apple develops an automobile, it will be a late mover in the car market.

BARRIERS TO ENTRY

Definition: Characteristics of a particular market that present difficulties for new firms trying to enter.

Sentence Example: Establishing reliable relationships with suppliers is a barrier to entry in any industry.

GRAND STRATEGY

Definition: A firm's comprehensive plan for integrating day-to-day operations in order to achieve its long term mission.

Sentence Example: Toyota's grand strategy encompasses the next 250 years.

FUNCTIONAL STRATEGIES

Definition: Plans for each of a firm's divisions or individual executives.

Sentence Example: Functional strategies for the marketing department included the installation of an inter-office mail system.

COMPANY CULTURE

Definition: The important assumptions shared by members of an organization and the experiences shared by employees in the work environment of a firm.

Sentence Example: The Christmas party was an important element of the company culture.

COMPANY MISSION

Definition: The unique purpose of a firm that sets it apart from other firms of its type.

Sentence Example: A PC in every home was the company mission of Microsoft.

COMPETITIVE POSITION
Definition: The statues that a firm wishes to achieve or has achieved within its industry.
Sentence Example: Google achieved its competitive position in the search market after eliminating Alta Vista.

DISTINCTIVE COMPETENCE
Definition: An expertise that provides a firm with a competitive advantage in the marketplace.
Sentence Example: Maytag's distinctive competence included excellent customer service for home washing machines.

COMPETITIVE REACTION
Definition: The reaction of competition to a firm's strategic initiatives.
Sentence Example: A new Android phone was Google's competitive reaction to Apple's iPhone 6.

BENCHMARKING
Definition: An analysis of strengths and weaknesses used to evaluate a firm's competitive position.
Sentence Example: Domino's wanted its thirty minute delivery time to become a benchmark against which other food delivery service was measured.

LEAPFROGGING

Definition: A product's rapid advance over its competition that creates an entirely new marketing space.

Sentence Example: The original Macintosh computer leapfrogged over the primitive word processing machines of the early 1980s.

MATURE INDUSTRY

Definition: An industry in decline, or growing slower than the overall economy.

Sentence Example: Laptop computers may soon be a mature industry as artificial intelligence continues to develop.

COST ADVANTAGE

Definition: An operating advantage enjoyed by an established firm, which can be difficult for entering firms to capture.

Sentence Example: Amazon has a significant cost advantage based on its volume of sales.

SUSTAINABLE COMPETITIVE ADVANTAGE

Definition: An advantage that can be maintained over a long period of time.

Sentence Example: Disney comic books had a sustainable competitive advantage over Atomic Bunny throughout the 1950s.

MACRO-ENVIRONMENT

Definition: All relevant forces outside a company's boundaries that can affect a company's business model strategies.

Sentence Example: The macro-environment of smartphone usage includes the possibility that phones can cause health problems.

DIFFERENTIATION STRATEGY

Definition: A strategy in which a firm strives to create and sell products and services that are unique in the marketplace.

Sentence Example: When it was first introduced, the Blackberry cell phone employed a powerful differentiation strategy.

DISTRIBUTION CHANNEL

Definition: The means by which products or services are moved from production to customer.

Sentence Example: Amazon's distribution channels may soon feature delivery by drones.

MATRIX ORGANIZATION

Definition: An organizational structure which delegates power to independent operating units which then rely on a centralized corporate facility for direction and support.

Sentence Example: The matrix of local debt collection offices were all in touch with the credit card office in South Dakota.

PORTFOLIO APPROACH

Definition: An organizational approach of looking at each division of a company as if it were a self-contained business in a total portfolio.

Sentence Example: At Google, the portfolio approach did not give first priority to the company's non-technical divisions.

STRATEGIC BUSINESS CLUSTERS

Definition: The organizational grouping of divisions in a business that serve similar strategic goals.

Sentence Example: Our strategic business cluster included marketing, R and D, and customer service.

VALUE CHAIN

Definition: Separate business processes that design, produce, market, deliver, and support a product or service.

Sentence Example: The value chain of the Home Depot store began and ended in the parking lot.

STRATEGIC ALLIANCES

Definition: Cooperative agreements between firms that go beyond normal communication but are short of a merger or joint venture partnership.

Sentence Example: The plumber formed a strategic alliance with the electrician in which customer referrals were rewarded with commissions.

HORIZONTAL INTEGRATION

Definition: The acquisition of a firm operating in a similar or supplemental area of business.

Sentence Example: Kellogg acquired and horizontally integrated Gardenburger, the first meat-free hamburger.

CONCENTRIC DIVERSIFICATION

Definition: A strategy of growth accomplished by acquiring firms that are different but synergistic with the acquiring firm.

Sentence Example: Through concentric diversification, Hormel acquired Applegate Farms, a producer of organic meat products.

E-Business

(DAY 17, DAY 29)

Welcome to our chapter on the vocabulary of E-business—an emerging commercial environment based on the elimination of brick and mortar reality. Consider Amazon.com. Jeff Bezos, the founder, had the great insight that his company's real product was the experience of *only* buying. In other words, the business of E-business is E-business. That's the underlying foundation for this chapter, and here are the key words.

1. E-business
2. E-tailing
3. Balanced scorecard
4. C2B
5. C2C
6. E-cash
7. Disruptive technologies
8. Bandwidth
9. ISP
10. Coherence design
11. Customer centric
12. Content management
13. Customization
14. HTML
15. EDI
16. FTP
17. PDF
18. Cyber rules
19. Internet governance
20. Intellectual property rights
21. Enterprise resource planning
22. Listserv
23. Bots
24. M-commerce
25. Digital representation

The following is a dialogue that would have been completely incomprehensible only a few years ago—like something out of science fiction. But the future is now.

*How is your **E-business** doing?*
We call it **E-tailing**, and it's going well actually. I've got a well-**balanced scorecard**.

*You're doing mainly **C2B**?*
Yes, and sometimes we have an online auction which I guess you could call **C2C**. We even use **E-cash** because I love **disruptive technologies**. But we do need more **bandwidth** from our **ISP**.

How have you designed your online presence?
We've emphasized **coherence design**, **customer centric content management** and we also facilitate **customization**. Everything seems to start with a C!

*How did you learn **HTML**, **EDI**, **FTP**, **PDF** and all the other tech stuff?*
The tech stuff is not that difficult but there are lots of **cyber rules** and regulations.

*Yes, **internet governance** and **intellectual property rights** are serious matters. What do you see in the future for retail E-business?*
I think **enterprise resource planning** will be important. **Listserv** and other **bots** will also play a role. **M-commerce**

will eventually become an everyday thing, and **digital representation** will take the place of just walking into a store.

....

E-BUSINESS

Definition: Internet commerce and the application of information technologies for internal or external business processes.

Sentence Example: E-businesses are making brick and mortar stores a thing of the past.

E-TAILING

Definition: A business model used by retail organizations for transactions online.

Sentence Example: Diamond rings don't lend themselves to e-tail selling.

BALANCED SCORECARD

Definition: A performance measurement tool that considers financial, marketing, and customer service perspectives.

Sentence Example: Mr. Blue's scorecard improved every month since bonuses became available.

C2B

Definition: Transactions between a consumer and a business.

Sentence Example: My college admissions counseling business was strictly C2B.

C2C
Definition: Transactions between a consumer and other consumers.
Sentence Example: The website facilitated C2C transactions among baseball card collectors.

E-CASH
Definition: Online tokens of value, including digital coins
Sentence Example: The bitcoin is an example of e-cash, or virtual currency.

DISRUPTIVE TECHNOLOGIES
Definition: Innovations that create new markets by introducing a new product or service, eventually disrupting and displacing existing markets and established companies.
Sentence Example: The cellphone is the most disruptive technology since the television set.

BANDWIDTH
Definition: The volume of data that a user can transmit or access over the Internet in a fixed period of time.
Sentence Example: Additional bandwidth can become expensive for highly developed websites.

ISP
Definition: An internet service provider is an organization or a company that has a permanent connection to the Internet and sells temporary connections its subscribers.
Sentence Example: The ISP of an internet user is easily traceable by law enforcement agencies.

COHERENCE DESIGN

Definition: An e-business approach that focuses on the alignment of strategy, task, structure, and user processes.

Sentence Example: Coherence design is the only alternative to chaos design for a fully developed online business.

CUSTOMER CENTRIC

Definition: A method of formalization and analysis of customer processes and agreements.

Sentence Example: Careful record keeping was the basis of the company's customer centric approach.

CONTENT MANAGEMENT

Definition: A systems-based approach for indexing digital content throughout its life cycle, including creation, storage, accessing and removal, including all platforms and mechanisms.

Sentence Example: Systems for content management vary according to industry and are especially critical for websites and libraries.

CUSTOMIZATION

Definition: A capability that allows website visitors to specify their own preferences.

Sentence Example: Website users love customization until it gets complicated.

HTML

Definition: Hyper Text Markup Language is the original coding scheme used for online documents.

Sentence Example: Some kindergartners are now more proficient in HTML than they are in English.

EDI
Definition: Electronic data interchange is the electronic exchange of data between computer systems and organizations in a standard format.
Sentence Example: The owner of the restaurant sent all his past tax returns to the IRS using EDI.

FTP
Definition: File transfer protocol is the Internet protocol for moving files online.
Sentence Example: The image was too dense for transmission by the standard file transfer protocol.

PDF
Definition: Portable document format or pdf is electronic document distribution in which files are viewed, navigated, and printed exactly as they were sent.
Sentence Example: A document in pdf form can't be edited unless converted to a word file or text.

CYBER RULES
Definition: Laws and regulations governing e-commerce.
Sentence Example: There are cyber rules governing the commercial use of copyrighted images.

INTERNET GOVERNANCE

Definition: Rules that affect the growth and development of the internet, including technical standards and policies.

Sentence Example: Internet governance involves many stakeholders, including governments, the private sector, and scientific, academic and technical institutions.

INTELLECTUAL PROPERTY RIGHTS

Definition: Laws covering literary and artistic works and other symbols, names, images and designs used in business.

Sentence Example: The attorney's specialty in intellectual property rights allowed him to join the country club.

ENTERPRISE RESOURCE PLANNING

Definition: A broad range of activities supported by application software to help manage business processes.

Sentence Example: The store's enterprise resource planning included a surveillance camera connected to the police department.

LISTSERV

Definition: An automatic emailing list server that sends messages to all individuals on a specific list.

Sentence Example: Listserv cost the non-profit business more contributions than it gained.

BOTS

Definition: Short for robots, BOTS are software programs given the specific task of locating and comparing products online.

Sentence Example: The bots had difficulty signing into many websites, but so did many people.

M-COMMERCE
Definition: Online commerce performed from mobile phones or tablets.
Sentence Example: Even M-commerce will become obsolete when cloud connections are built into the walls.

DIGITAL REPRESENTATION
Definition: Denotes the absence of physical contact in a virtual market, which can be a barrier to purchasing.
Sentence Example: Digital representations may become an everyday experience as the technology of holograms advances.

Human Resources
HIRING AND FIRING
(DAY 18, DAY 29)

The term Human Resources appeared in the 1960s, replacing what used to be called "personnel." As issues of diversity, compensation, and advancement have become more prominent, the terminology of HR is not just useful, but essential to know. This chapter is a brief introduction, focuses on hiring and firing. If you do the first one right, you won't have to do the second. That's the goal.

1. Adverse impact
2. Protected class
3. Jobs-as-property doctrine
4. Affirmative action
5. Arbitration agreements
6. Mass layoffs
7. Plant closing
8. Behavior-based interviewing
9. High-potential hires
10. Measurable standards
11. Assessment traps
12. Chat traps
13. Self-disclosure technique
14. Continuing the paragraph
15. Amplified reflection
16. Agreement with a twist
17. Confidence ruler
18. Employment-at-will
19. For-cause termination
20. Bundling offenses
21. De minimis infraction
22. Double-sided reflection
23. Constructive discharge
24. Qualified privilege
25. Separation agreement

As the following conversation suggests, issues of hiring and firing are an area of business vocabulary where humor seems to play no part. This has become a sensitive focus in an era when disputes can lead to expensive litigation.

*Does the term "**adverse impact**" have a special meaning in HR issues?*

Yes, it does. Adverse impact refers specifically to negative effects of employment practices on **protected classes**. It can also refer to the effects of non-employment, or failure to offer employment, that could be covered by the **jobs-as-property doctrine**.

*So that would include groups of people that are covered by **affirmative action**.*

That's right. But it could also refer to groups covered by **arbitration agreements** or **mass layoffs** or **plant closings**, which also have specific definitions.

I see. But those are large scale situations that deal with substantial numbers of people. I'm sure there can also be adverse impact issues for individual employees.

That's definitely true. And we want to head off those issues as soon as possible, starting with the interview process.

What are some of the important principles and techniques in that process?

Well, **behavior-based interviewing** is the foundation of everything else. You look at the candidate's history in order to identify **high-potential hires**. You also try to clarify the **measurable**

standards that will be in place from the start of the hire. You want to avoid things like **assessment traps** or **chat traps** in an interview, but **self-disclosure** can be a good interviewing technique when it inspires disclosure by the candidate.

I suppose you don't want to make it obvious that you're using particular techniques.

Definitely not. For example, an interviewing technique called **continuing the paragraph** can be useful, but you have to be sure you're not putting words in the candidate's mouth. That's also true with techniques like **amplified reflection** or the one I call **agreement with a twist**. I often end an interview by asking a candidate to describe his **confidence ruler** for different responsibilities of the job.

*What about a termination process? That must be even more complicated than hiring, especially if the relationship is something other than **employment-at-will**.*

A **for-cause termination** process usually takes place over a sustained period of time. Once it's clear that there's a problem, you can start **bundling offenses**. This can include everything from *de minimis* infractions to more serious matters. There can be a meeting that includes some **double-sided reflection**. Some employers try to orchestrate a **constructive discharge**, which can simplify things if it works.

What are the final steps?

The final steps could include a discussion of **qualified privilege**, and then the signing of a **formal separation agreement**. After that, it starts all over again by hiring someone else.

ADVERSE IMPACT

Definition: The negative effects of a company's employment practices, including practices that unfavorably affect a protected group.

Sentence Example: The absence of handicapped parking spaces had an adverse impact on the store's ability to hire qualified personnel.

PROTECTED CLASS

Definition: A group of people who are legally protected from discrimination and harassment, including discrimination based on race, religion, and disability.

Sentence Example: Sexual orientation may constitute a protected class in some workplace situations.

JOB AS PROPERTY DOCTRINE

Definition: A legal theory asserting that work is an intrinsic right of American citizens, and that that work should not be denied arbitrarily or without just cause.

Sentence Example: The jobs as property doctrine sounds interesting, but it's difficult to assert in an actual interview.

AFFIRMATIVE ACTION

Definition: Practices in hiring or education intended to improve the prospects of groups that have not been given equal opportunities in the past.

Sentence Example: Some important legal decisions concerning affirmative action have involved admission to the University of Texas.

ARBITRATION AGREEMENT

Definition: An agreement between an employer and employee to use a third party authority to resolve work-related disputes.

Sentence Example: Mr. Green's employment contract included an arbitration agreement that referenced a well-known attorney.

MASS LAYOFF

Definition: Legally, the loss of at least fifty full-time employees or least 33 percent of the full-time employees at a single site of employment.

Sentence Example: The Wham-o Company instituted a mass layoff when hula hoops suddenly lost popularity.

PLANT CLOSING

Definition: Layoff of fifty or more employees at a single location over a thirty-day period for a period of at least six months.

Sentence Example: The plant closing by US Steel on the South Side of Chicago hurt the local economy, but improved the air quality.

BEHAVIOR-BASED INTERVIEWING

Definition: An interviewing technique that emphasizes and analyzes a candidate's past actions and experiences.

Sentence Example: Behavior-based interviewing must remember that past performance does not guarantee future results.

HIGH-POTENTIAL HIRE

Definition: A new employee who will stay with the company, add to the company's skills base, progress through the ranks, and provide the company with an excellent return on investment.

Sentence Example: Both candidates seemed like high potential hires but only one was bi-lingual.

MEASURABLE STANDARD

Definition: An expectation of work responsibilities that is specific, quantifiable, and clearly communicated in advance.

Sentence Example: The expectation that all employees would be in their cubicles at 8:00 AM was a clear and measurable standard.

ASSESSMENT TRAP

Definition: The error of overvaluing tests and other information about candidates at the cost of not listening closely to the candidate themselves.

Sentence Example: The National Football League's intelligence test for new players is potentially an assessment trap.

CHAT TRAP

Definition: The error of engaging a candidate in informal talk that does not advance the most important aspects of the interview process.

Sentence Example: With the Super Bowl only a week away, the interview fell into a chat trap of football talk.

SELF-DISCLOSURE TECHNIQUE

Definition: An interviewer's sharing of facts and anecdotes about himself or herself in the expectation that a candidate will do the same.

Sentence Example: As an example of self-disclosure, the interviewer mentioned a large fish he had caught.

CONTINUING THE PARAGRAPH

Definition: A method of reflective listening in which the counselor follows up something the candidate has said with what might be the client's next, as yet unspoken sentence or paragraph.

Sentence Example: When the candidate began to describe climbing up a mountain, I continued his paragraph with a description of climbing down.

AMPLIFIED REFLECTION

Definition: A response in which the interviewer reflects back a candidate's statements with greater intensity than the candidate had expressed

Sentence Example: Jim's amplified reflection of Kevin's idea inspired Kevin to share more details.

AGREEMENT WITH A TWIST

Definition: An affirmation of a client's content, followed by a reframing or other comment.

Sentence Example: My response to Peter's assertion that he could have been a professional baseball player was agreement with a twist.

CONFIDENCE RULER

Definition: An imaginary scale from 1 to 10 on which candidates are asked to rate their level of confidence or ability.

Sentence Example: On a confidence ruler of 1 to 10, the candidate rated himself at 11 with regard to programming.

EMPLOYMENT-AT-WILL

Definition: A contractual relationships in which an employee can be dismissed by an employer for any reason and without warning.

Sentence Example: In most states, employment-at-will is the most common work agreement.

TERMINATION FOR CAUSE

Definition: The dismissal of an employee for a severe error in action or judgment.

Sentence Example: The vice-president was terminated for cause when he sent an email to the wrong person.

BUNDLING OFFENSES

Definition: Documenting an employee's poor performance by creating a dated ledger of incidents.

Sentence Example: Mr. Potter's specialty was bundling offenses, especially around Christmas time.

DE MINIMIS INFRACTION

Definition: A minor error that by itself is not normally a cause for termination.

Sentence Example: The joke Norman told in the crowded elevator was considered a de minimis infraction.

DOUBLE-SIDED REFLECTION

Definition: An interviewer reflection that includes agreement followed by another point of view.

Sentence Example: The interviewer responded to the client with a double-sided reflection on the topic of air travel.

CONSTRUCTIVE DISCHARGE

Definition: An employer who make the workplace conditions so unpleasant that the employee is compelled to leave.

Sentence Example: As an aspect of his constructive discharge, Roger did not receive any emails for twelve straight days.

QUALIFIED PRIVILEGE

Definition: A legal doctrine that protects employers from defamation claims when providing references for a terminated employee to other companies.

Sentence Example: Qualified privilege means that former employers must limit their comments to interests shared by a prospective employer.

SEPARATION AGREEMENT

Definition: A release form signed by an employee who is being terminated that describes any extra compensation the employee will receive for not making any claims against the company.

Sentence Example: My very generous separation agreement prevented me from filing a lawsuit, although I desperately wanted to do so.

Leadership

(DAY 19, DAY 30)

Back in 2008, the legendary former CEO of the Chrysler Corporation, Lee Iacocca, wrote a book with a provocative title: *Where Have All the Leaders Gone?* The title was attention-grabbing, but it was certainly not challenging the status quo. Indeed, the lament about the "lack of strong leadership" in the culture, and the business world in particular, had been a common refrain for some time and still is. But, there is a axiom, attributed to the philosopher Aristotle, which says "Nature abhors a vacuum." The vacuum of strong leadership is going to produce an increasing demand for more leaders in all of the arenas in which business operates. Indeed, the topic of leadership is now one of the most closely studied aspects of business success, with its own increasingly technical vocabulary. Here are the words and phrases relating to leadership.

1. Attribution theory
2. Cognitive resource theory
3. Cooperation theory
4. Expectancy theory
5. Path-goal theory
6. Compliance
7. Coercive power
8. Concert building
9. Behavior shaping
10. Behavior modification
11. Congruence
12. Conjunctive communication
13. Consultative leader
14. Disjunctive communication
15. Internal locus of control
16. Self-efficacy
17. Servant leader
18. Expertise approach

19. Expert power
20. Leadership polarity
21. Charismatic
22. Socialized charismatic

23. Personalized charismatic
24. Contingency leadership
25. Persuade package
26. Lateral thinking

....

This conversation might save you some tuition expenses in business school. The dialogue explores leadership issues from the current scientific perspective. It is not enough to be Henry Ford or the Wright Brothers anymore. Today's business leaders need to be psychologists as well as engineers or marketers. This dialogue will show you how that sounds.

What's taught in business schools about management and leadership is usually a lot simpler than it sounds. It's just giving fancy names to simple concepts.

Can you give me some examples?

*Sure. **Attribution theory** means finding a cause for something. You give credit or blame to somebody who does something. There are a lot more theories: **cognitive resource theory**, **cooperation theory**, **expectancy theory**, and **path-goal theory**. Do you want more?*

I think that's enough for now.

*The purpose of all those theories is to gain **compliance**, which can be done positively or negatively—with **coercive power** or **concert building**. Psychologists refer to both of those as **behavior shaping**.*

Is that the same as **behavior modification**?

Not exactly. Behavior modification is a more general term. But I suppose any technique really depends on the talents and capabilities of the manager.

Sure. But you have to be able to communicate those talents and capabilities. That involves a lot of variables, so you want to be as **congruent** *and* **conjunctive** *as possible. I also believe in* **consultative leadership**, *but not everyone does.*
Is there such a thing as **disjunctive communication**?

Yes, that term does exist but it's something you want to avoid. As a manager, I try to convince people that they have their own **internal locus of control**, *which is another highbrow term. It's just a way of building a sense of* **self-efficacy**.
That sounds like the very popular concept of **servant leadership**.

Yes, that's what it is. But servant leadership works best when there's an **expertise approach** *backed up by* **expert power**.
Do you think you're well-liked by your teams?

I hope so, but there's always going to be some **leadership polarity**. *You can't please everybody all of the time. I try to be* **charismatic**, *but I want to be a* **socialized charismatic** *rather than a* **personalized charismatic**. *Regardless of the details, a* **contingency leadership** *generally works best.*
Can you summarize what that means?

*It means no two people are the same and no two situations are the same. You need a well-thought-out **persuade package**, and plenty of **lateral thinking**.*

....

ATTRIBUTION THEORY
Definition: The idea that everything has an identifiable cause and that for most things there is someone to blame.
Sentence Example: We discussed the events leading up to Pearl Harbor in terms of attribution theory.

COGNITIVE RESOURCE THEORY
Definition: An explanation of leadership based on the leader's ability to remain calm under stress.
Sentence Example: The CEO's performance during the product recall was a clear confirmation of cognitive resource theory.

COOPERATION THEORY
Definition: Any adaptation that has evolved, at least in part, to increase the reproductive success of the actor's social partners.
Sentence Example: A great and happy marriage of two individuals who grow in their love for one another, and also produce happy and well-adjusted children is a demonstration of cooperation theory.

EXPECTANCY THEORY

Definition: A theory that people's effort depends on the amount of reward they can expect in return.

Sentence Example: As a believer in expectancy theory, the professor offered to buy yogurt for the highest achieving students.

PATH-GOAL THEORY

Definition: An explanation of leadership that specifically references what effective leaders must do in a variety of situations.

Sentence Example: Path-goal theory explained why President Kennedy frequently napped during the Cuban Missile Crisis.

COMPLIANCE

Definition: A minimum level of success achieved by the leader of a group.

Sentence Example: The sales manager expected top results, not just compliance, from all the reps.

COERCIVE POWER

Definition: The authority to use punishment or the threat of punishment to influence performance.

Sentence Example: Coercive power can sometimes be an effective management technique, but only in the short term.

CONCERT BUILDING

Definition: A leadership style based on creating consensus and agreement among as many people as possible.

Sentence Example: Concert building is a very different leadership style from the military's traditional chain of command.

BEHAVIOR SHAPING

Definition: Rewarding behavior that aligns with the leader's expectations and adjusting the reward as the behavior improves or degrades.

Sentence Example: The teacher was able to shape the students' behavior by pasting gold stars on their test papers.

BEHAVIOR MODIFICATION

Definition: Any attempt by a leader to change behavior by manipulating rewards and punishment.

Sentence Example: Behavior modification is always taking place, whether or not a leader is aware of it.

CONGRUENCE

Definition: A leadership style that closely matches words and actions.

Sentence Example: There was congruence between my supervisor's promise of a raise and its appearance in my next paycheck.

CONJUNCTIVE COMMUNICATION
Definition: Messages that proceed logically and without contradiction from previous messages.
Sentence Example: Conjunctive communication is essential for building a team's loyalty and morale.

CONSULTATIVE LEADER
Definition: A manager who confers with others before taking action.
Sentence Example: John Kennedy was better known as a consultative leader than was Lyndon Johnson.

DISJUNCTIVE COMMUNICATION
Definition: Communication that seems disconnected or contradictory to preceding messages.
Sentence Example: The new boss's disjunctive communications led to confusion about the assignment of parking spaces.

INTERNAL LOCUS OF CONTROL
Definition: The belief that you yourself are the primary cause of success or lack of success in your life.
Sentence Example: It's often easier to blame external forces than to accept oneself as an internal locus of control.

SELF-EFFICACY
Definition: Confidence in your ability to carry out a specific task or assignment.
Sentence Example: The runner's sense of self-efficacy was the key to her completing the marathon.

SERVANT LEADER

Definition: A leader who sees himself or herself as working on behalf of a team, rather than to further self-interest.

Sentence Example: The concept of the servant leader has inspired several books on corporate management.

EXPERTISE APPROACH

Definition: Belief that a leader's responsibility includes identifying an area of expertise that creates competitive advantage.

Sentence Example: The late Thomas Watson of IBM saw mainframe computing as the basis of the company's expertise approach.

EXPERT POWER

Definition: A leader's ability to influence others based on his or her personal knowledge, skills, or abilities.

Sentence Example: The expert power of the orchestra conductor was obvious when he began to play the French horn.

LEADERSHIP POLARITY

Definition: The fact that leaders tend to be either strongly admired or deeply unpopular.

Sentence Example: During the Great Depression, the public's view of Franklin Roosevelt exemplified leadership polarity.

CHARISMATIC

Definition: An inborn energy that a leader naturally communicates to other people, with the effect that others want to be in the leader's presence and do as the leader says.

Sentence Example: Steve Jobs was both a highly charismatic leader and a grown man who sometimes acted like a spoiled child.

SOCIALIZED CHARISMATIC

Definition: A leader who uses his or her talents primarily to benefit others.

Sentence Example: As socialized charismatics, several of the early American presidents were broke when they left office.

PERSONALIZED CHARISMATIC

Definition: A leader whose primary motivation is personal self-interest.

Sentence Example: Commodore Vanderbilt was a personalized charismatic who wanted to erect a solid gold statue of himself.

CONTINGENCY LEADERSHIP

Definition: The belief that leaders are most effective when they adjust their behavior to situational forces, including characteristics of group members.

Sentence Example: The basketball coach's leadership style was contingent on the motivation of his players.

PERSUADE PACKAGE

Definition: A standardized set of leadership tactics that influences a group in a particular way.

Sentence Example: Theodore Roosevelt's persuade package included speaking softly and carrying a big stick.

LATERAL THINKING

Definition: An expansive thinking process that attempts to find unique and unexpected solutions to problems.

Sentence Example: Einstein's linking of space and time was a successful use of lateral thinking.

Remote Working

(DAY 20, DAY 30)

Welcome to the final chapter of our book on business vocabulary. As of the writing of this chapter, the world is undergoing the COVID-19 pandemic of historic proportions. Regardless of how long the pandemic persists, economic forecasters envision many changes for businesses worldwide. Some of those changes will be completely new and previously unforeseen, while others will be the acceleration of trends that were already underway. The topic of "remote working" fits the latter description—this trend was well underway prior to the pandemic, and is likely to become more prevalent and familiar to even more businesses (and the businesses you serve and collaborate with) in the years to come.

1. Asynchronous communication
2. Brick-and-mortar business
3. Collaboration tools
4. Co-located company
5. Connectivity
6. Co-working
7. Digital nomad
8. Digital workplace
9. Distributed Work
10. F2F
11. Gig worker
12. Hybrid teams
13. Loungewear
14. Off-site meeting
15. Remote working / teleworking
16. Scrum meeting
17. Synchronous communication
18. Video call
19. Work-in-place
20. Work-from-home

The following vignette dramatizes what was likely taking place in many workplaces during the 2020 pandemic, and will continue to occur for many years afterward. It begins with Annette Martin, the President of a company we'll call ABC Communications, making a company-wide address to all employees via online video (Zoom, Skype or similar online meeting service). In her talk Annette discusses the changes the company had to make as a result of the COVID-19 Pandemic, and how this would involve working remotely for the near future. Following that address, two employees of ABC, Noah and Justina, have a separate phone discussion about what the president's address means for their careers.

Annette Martin: Good morning ABC Team and thank you for joining me on this **video call**. There's an English expression, supposedly a translation of a Chinese curse, "May you live in interesting times." Those words have never been more relevant than now. For some of us, I'm sure these times feel closer to a curse—but I want to convince you that many of the changes we are going through as an organization are not just interesting; they are an opportunity for growth. First, I want to thank the team for how well you have adjusted to **working-from-home**, despite the occasional distractions you have in your home environment, and the occasional issues some of our employees have had with **connectivity.** While we are still trying to deal with all the issues raised by our rapid switch to working virtually, rest assured that the lessons we are learning are extraordinarily valuable.

Why? Because learning how to **work remotely** is the wave of the future. And we are not simply talking about working from home, but about the many ways for engaging in an entirely **digital workplace,** such as working with **hybrid teams** and **co-working**. I don't want to start any unnecessary rumors—we still plan to keep our **brick-and-mortar business** for several years to come. But, I believe that we can work on these two tracks at the same time—and this experience, when we are forced to **telework,** provides an opportunity to explore new ways of making our work more flexible. Later this week, I'll be gathering at an **off-site meeting** with a group of selected employees and experts in working remotely to discuss next steps. Thank you to our team members for your time. I wanted everyone to receive this **synchronous Communication** so we're all on the same page. For those not present and for whom this message will be an **asynchronous Communication**, we are sending a link to the recording so you can hear me directly. Please share the link with any of your direct reports who are not here today. In the meantime, stay safe and let's continue to produce great results—wherever you're working today!

After the video call, ABC employees Noah and Justina immediately call to discuss what the President's message might mean for them.

Noah: Well, Justina, to paraphrase Annette that was certainly an "interesting" call. What the heck do you think that means? Am I going to be working from my messy, home office for the rest of my life? I don't mind doing that once in a while, but gosh, if I wanted that life, I would have been a freelancer! I'm the kind of person who needs to have an **F2F** meeting once in a while—it helps with my creativity and engagement.

Justina: Hey, look at the bright side! You get to go to work in **loungewear** for the rest of your life! Seriously, I think she was saying that they're looking at transitioning to a **work-in-place** policy, not necessarily a 100% **work-from-home** policy.

Noah: What's the difference?

Justina: It's where you can work in another location—and that could be working-from-home, but it could also be another co-working facility where you share space with other employees, or it could be a **distributed work** model where there are multiple satellite offices, apart from the central home office. Heck, I have friends who work at companies whose model is totally virtual. There's no central office—the team is in different, smaller offices around the country. While they don't get the opportunity for a lot of **F2F** meetings, they do have regular **Scrum meetings** on a daily basis to stay connected.

Noah: You mean I could be like one of those **digital nomads** who's free to travel the world, taking my work with me? I like that idea! Working at a coffee shop adjacent to the Eiffel Tower would be nice!

Justina: Nice try! I don't think they're going to make you a world traveler just yet. For now, I think you'll just be working from home more often. They will put all of our files into the **Cloud**, and set us up with some **collaboration tools** to help us manage our projects with people who are not working with us physically.

Noah: Hey, even if I'm working remotely, as long as they treat me as a professional member of the team, and not some glorified **Gig worker**, it does sound "interesting."

....

ASYNCHRONOUS COMMUNICATION
Definition: The transmission or relay of information with a time lag. Examples include online learning, discussion forums and e-mail.
Sentence Example: The online course from the professor was a form of asynchronous communication, allowing students to learn at their own pace.

BRICK-AND-MORTAR BUSINESS
Definition: A business with a workplace environment at a physical office.
Sentence Example: These dot.com businesses do not carry inventory, and most of them do not have a brick-and-mortar business environment.

COLLABORATION TOOLS

Definition: A technology tool that can be used to help people work together to achieve a common goal or objective.

Sentence Example: ABC Communications has provided a range of collaboration tools to help their team create an effective public relations campaign for their client.

CO-LOCATED COMPANY

Definition: The placement of several (sometimes related) business entities within the same location.

Sentence Example: The Company's many components were designed with the key suppliers at ABC Designs, a co-located company at headquarters.

CONNECTIVITY

Definition: Computing capacity for connection to the internet, as well as the interconnection of platforms, systems, networks and applications.

Sentence Example: These reports expanded the analysis to include not only computers and modems, but also internet connectivity.

CO-WORKING

Definition: An arrangement by which employees working for various companies or self-employed individuals share an office or other workspace.

Sentence Example: Many of these different organizations get together in co-working spaces around the campus.

DIGITAL NOMAD

Definition: Digital nomads are remote workers who usually travel to different locations. They often work in coffee shops, co-working spaces, or public libraries, relying on devices with wireless internet capabilities like smart phones and mobile hotspots to do their work wherever they want.

Sentence Example: Personally, as an employee, I like to be "rooted" in one place, but my friend John is a true Digital Nomad—he likes to work anywhere around the world that has a Wi-Fi connection.

DIGITAL WORKPLACE

Definition: The virtual equivalent of a physical workplace.

Sentence Example: As a management team, we must proactively develop a digital workplace that coordinates the technology, process and people aspects.

DISTRIBUTED WORK

Definition: Work where the entire team is geographically distributed, usually without a central physical office.

Sentence Example: Distributed work can be very successful, if the company displays technology readiness. Otherwise, you will run into problems, such as complaints about the quality of communication over audio and video conferencing.

F2F

Definition: An abbreviation of "Face-to-Face," usually to refer to a type of meeting that you have less often when working remotely.

Sentence Example: I got a brand new suit because I have an F2F interview later today, and I want to make a good impression.

GIG WORKER

Definition: Gig workers are independent contractors, online platform workers, contract firm workers, on-call workers and temporary workers. Gig workers enter into formal agreements with on-demand companies to provide services to the company's clients.

Sentence Example: I needed some extra income while I'm working through college, so I decided to become a Gig worker for Uber Eats. It's nice because I can take Gigs when I have time by indicating when I'm available, so I can work when I'm done with my studies.

HYBRID TEAMS

Definition: A team in which some individuals work in the same location, and other members work remotely.

Sentence Example: We have a hybrid team working to help design and publish your book. The editors and proofreaders work here in our corporate office, while the designers of the interior and exterior work remotely.

LOUNGEWEAR

Definition: Casual, comfortable clothing suitable for wearing at home.

Sentence Example: One of the benefits of working-from-home is swapping pants, suits and starchy dress shirts for sweatpants and other types of loungewear.

OFF-SITE MEETING

Definition: A meeting that happens outside of the offices, at a new, and often distant, destination, usually at a co-working facility, hotel, or rented conference room.

Sentence Example: Our management team needs to get away from the home office, and from the daily distractions of work, and do our strategic planning at an off-site meeting place.

REMOTE WORK / TELEWORK

Definition: The practice of working-from-home or another remote location, making use of the internet, e-mail and telephone.

Sentence Example: More than half of the respondents polled stated that they do consider requirements associated with telework when they are making decisions about IT infrastructure.

SCRUM MEETING

Definition: A very short meeting (often held daily) in which team members efficiently answer three questions: What did I accomplish yesterday? What do I plan to accomplish today? Do I see any blocks that might prevent me from accomplishing my goal?

Sentence Example: When I'm working remotely, I really appreciate our department's scrum meeting, since it helps keep me focused and motivated.

SYNCHRONOUS COMMUNICATION

Definition: Defined as "real-time" communication between people. Examples include face-to-face, phone, video and "chat" communication.

Sentence Example: In the sales profession, I always recommend that you present and negotiate with customers using some kind of synchronous communication, so you can engage their reactions and objections in real-time.

VIDEO CALL

Definition: A phone call using an Internet connection that uses video, allowing the callers to see each other as they talk. Calls are made with mobile phones or tablets with a camera and a screen, or with a computer's webcam.

Sentence Example: There are many great types of video call services you can choose—Skype, Zoom, and Face-Time are all good options.

WORK-IN-PLACE

Definition: A work arrangement in which employees primarily work from locations of their choice instead of the company's central brick-and-mortar office.

Sentence Example: The great part about this project is that the team members don't have to come into the home office to complete it; the company has given all of the employees the green light to work-in-place so we can get it done quickly.

WORK-FROM-HOME

Definition: A work arrangement in which the employee primarily works from a home office instead of the company's central brick-and-mortar office.

Sentence Example: The Company's new policy is that those who have worked at the company for five years or longer, and have had consistently strong performance reviews, may work-from-home at least twice per week.

Congratulations! You've come to the end of our *30 Day Program* to improve your business vocabulary. Now it's time to start putting these words and phrases to use. Some of them are humorous, others are rather technical—but they will make an impression if you put them into action. Toward that end, it will help to review this book more than once. This vocabulary should become a working part of your professional identity. This is word power in a true and lasting sense, much more than just a dead cat bounce. You do remember the definition of dead cat bounce, don't you?

Thank you for your time and attention. I hope you've enjoyed the book. Good luck and best wishes for success in everything you do.

Appendix
THE 30 DAY PROGRAM WORKSHEET

FIRST INTENSIVE LESSONS
DAY 1 THROUGH DAY 20

Day 1:

Banking and Finance, Part One

Read Chapter_____

Read Out Loud_____

Intentional Review_____

Bedtime Review_____

Day 2:

Banking and Finance, Part Two

Read Chapter_____

Read Out Loud_____

Intentional Review_____

Bedtime Review_____

Day 3:

Banking and Finance, Part Three

Read Chapter_____

Read Out Loud_____

Intentional Review_____

Bedtime Review_____

Day 4:

Banking and Finance, Part Four

Read Chapter_____

Read Out Loud_____

Intentional Review_____

Bedtime Review_____

Day 5:

Negotiation, Part One

Read Chapter_____

Read Out Loud_____

Intentional Review_____

Bedtime Review_____

Day 6:

Negotiation, Part Two

Read Chapter_____

Read Out Loud_____

Intentional Review_____

Bedtime Review_____

Day 7:

Negotiation, Part Three

Read Chapter_____

Read Out Loud_____

Intentional Review_____

Bedtime Review_____

Day 8:

Negotiation, Part Four

Read Chapter_____

Read Out Loud_____

Intentional Review_____

Bedtime Review_____

Day 9:

Marketing, Part One

Read Chapter_____

Read Out Loud_____

Intentional Review_____

Bedtime Review_____

Day 10:

Marketing, Part Two

Read Chapter_____

Read Out Loud_____

Intentional Review_____

Bedtime Review_____

Day 11:

Marketing, Part Three

Read Chapter_____

Read Out Loud_____

Intentional Review_____

Bedtime Review_____

Day 12:

Marketing, Part Four

Read Chapter_____

Read Out Loud_____

Intentional Review_____

Bedtime Review_____

Day 13:
Sales, Part One

Read Chapter_____

Read Out Loud_____

Intentional Review_____

Bedtime Review_____

Day 14:
Sales, Part Two

Read Chapter_____

Read Out Loud_____

Intentional Review_____

Bedtime Review_____

Day 15:
Entrepreneurship, Part One

Read Chapter_____

Read Out Loud_____

Intentional Review_____

Bedtime Review_____

Day 16:
Entrepreneurship, Part Two

Read Chapter_____

Read Out Loud_____

Intentional Review_____

Bedtime Review_____

Day 17:
E-Business

Read Chapter_____

Read Out Loud_____

Intentional Review_____

Bedtime Review_____

Day 18:
Human Resources: Hiring and Firing

Read Chapter_____

Read Out Loud_____

Intentional Review_____

Bedtime Review_____

Day 19:
Leadership

Read Chapter_____

Read Out Loud_____

Intentional Review_____

Bedtime Review_____

Day 20:
Remote Working

Read Chapter_____

Read Out Loud_____

Intentional Review_____

Bedtime Review_____

ESSENTIAL REVIEW
DAY 21 THROUGH DAY 30

Day 21:

Banking and Finance, Part One

Read Chapter_____

Read Out Loud_____

Intentional Review_____

Bedtime Review_____

Day 21:

Banking and Finance, Part Two

Read Chapter_____

Read Out Loud_____

Intentional Review_____

Bedtime Review_____

Day 22:

Banking and Finance, Part Three

Read Chapter_____

Read Out Loud_____

Intentional Review_____

Bedtime Review_____

Day 22:

Banking and Finance, Part Four

Read Chapter_____

Read Out Loud_____

Intentional Review_____

Bedtime Review_____

Day 23:

Negotiation, Part One

Read Chapter_____

Read Out Loud_____

Intentional Review_____

Bedtime Review_____

Day 23:

Negotiation, Part Two

Read Chapter_____

Read Out Loud_____

Intentional Review_____

Bedtime Review_____

Day 24:

Negotiation, Part Three

Read Chapter_____

Read Out Loud_____

Intentional Review_____

Bedtime Review_____

Day 24:

Negotiation, Part Four

Read Chapter_____

Read Out Loud_____

Intentional Review_____

Bedtime Review_____

Day 25:

Marketing, Part One

Read Chapter_____

Read Out Loud_____

Intentional Review_____

Bedtime Review_____

Day 25:

Marketing, Part Two

Read Chapter_____

Read Out Loud_____

Intentional Review_____

Bedtime Review_____

Day 26:

Marketing, Part Three

Read Chapter_____

Read Out Loud_____

Intentional Review_____

Bedtime Review_____

Day 26:

Marketing, Part Four

Read Chapter_____

Read Out Loud_____

Intentional Review_____

Bedtime Review_____

Day 27:

Sales, Part One

Read Chapter_____

Read Out Loud_____

Intentional Review_____

Bedtime Review_____

Day 27:

Sales, Part Two

Read Chapter_____

Read Out Loud_____

Intentional Review_____

Bedtime Review_____

Day 28:
Entrepreneurship, Part One

Read Chapter_____

Read Out Loud_____

Intentional Review_____

Bedtime Review_____

Day 28:
Entrepreneurship, Part Two

Read Chapter_____

Read Out Loud_____

Intentional Review_____

Bedtime Review_____

Day 29:
E-Business

Read Chapter_____

Read Out Loud_____

Intentional Review_____

Bedtime Review_____

Day 29:
**Human Resources:
Hiring and Firing**

Read Chapter_____

Read Out Loud_____

Intentional Review_____

Bedtime Review_____

Day 30:
Leadership

Read Chapter_____

Read Out Loud_____

Intentional Review_____

Bedtime Review_____

Day 30:
Remote Working

Read Chapter_____

Read Out Loud_____

Intentional Review_____

Bedtime Review_____

Word and Phrase Index